Desert Gardening for Beginners

Desert Gardening for Beginners

How to Grow Vegetables, Flowers and Herbs in an Arid Climate

Cathy Cromell, Linda A. Guy and Lucy K. Bradley

Illustrations by Erin O'Dell

Cover Photos and Design by Joanne Littlefield

Arizona Master Gardener Press
in cooperation with The University of Arizona
Maricopa County Cooperative Extension

Printed in the United States of America

12 11 10   6 5 4

Publisher's Cataloging in Publication
(Provided by Quality Books, Inc.)

Cromell, Cathy.
    Desert gardening for beginners : how to grow
    vegetables, flowers and herbs in an arid climate /
    Cathy Cromell, Linda A. Guy and Lucy K. Bradley ;
    illustrations by Erin O'Dell. — 1st ed.
      p. cm.
    Includes bibliographical references and index.
    LCCN: 99-072759
    ISBN: 0-9651987-2-3

    1. Desert gardening—Southwest, New. 2. Arid
regions plants—Southwest, New. I. Guy, Linda
A. II. Bradley, Lucy K. III. Title

    SB427.5.C76 1999   635'.9525
                     QBI99-535

Some of the material in this book appeared in *Success With School Gardens: How to Create a Learning Oasis in the Desert* by the same authors.

Issued in furtherance of Cooperative Extension work, acts of May 8 and June 30, 1914, in cooperation with the U.S. Department of Agriculture, James A. Christenson, Director, Cooperative Extension, College of Agriculture, The University of Arizona.
The University of Arizona College of Agriculture is an equal opportunity employer authorized to provide research, educational information and other services only to individuals and institutions that function without regard to sex, race, religion, color, national origin, age, Vietnam Era Veteran's status, or disability.
Any products, services, or organizations that are mentioned, shown, or indirectly implied in this publication do not imply endorsement by The University of Arizona.

Arizona Master Gardener Press
Phoenix, Arizona 85040

Table of Contents

Introduction

esert gardening *is* different. Bookstore shelves are lined with colorful volumes that describe gardening methods suitable for other areas of the country, but following that advice spells disaster for low-desert gardeners. We contend with alkaline soils and water, extreme heat, a relentless sun and minimal rainfall. On the other hand, temperatures sometimes dip below freezing and we experience frosts. New residents to the Southwest often attempt to bring their gardening methods and plants with them and are often disappointed when tomatoes planted in June don't bear fruit or favorite plants that thrived "back home" soon turn yellow and die.

Desert Gardening for Beginners: How to Grow Vegetables, Flowers and Herbs in an Arid Climate includes information that you need to be a successful gardener in the Southwest. In an easy-to-understand format, we show you how to select a garden site, prepare the soil, make compost, choose appropriate plants, fertilize, manage pests, water effectively and more. If you are a newcomer to the desert or have never gardened before, all the information you need to grow healthy plants is here. If you are an experienced gardener, you will still find useful information and perhaps a few new ideas to try in your garden.

The basic concepts in this book, such as improving the soil, watering methods and pest management, apply whether you want to plant vegetables, flowers or herbs. If you follow these guidelines you'll be able to grow any combination of these annual plants successfully. In addition, there's a separate chapter with specific pointers on vegetables, flowers and herbs.

Many newcomers are confused by the desert's seasons, not realizing that we enjoy both a cool- and warm-weather growing season, with different plants thriving in each. (Yes, tomatoes do grow well here, but they must be planted in early spring, not June!) The appendices include calendars that will help you determine the best time to plant.

You'll soon join the ranks of experienced gardeners who know how lucky we are to live in the low desert—where something can be planted or harvested year-round.

Welcome to desert gardening!

Where to Locate Your Garden

As you check out possible garden sites, remember that location is the most important factor in establishing a successful garden. Favorable sunlight, relatively level ground, access to water, good drainage and decent soil are the critical elements to consider, all of which will be described below. Poor soil can be improved, but a poor location is forever a poor location!

Sunlight

Most guidance regarding sun exposure on seed packets or in gardening books is not very useful in the desert, with its intense sunlight and wildly fluctuating daily temperatures. Through experience, you will begin to appreciate the lighting needs of individual plants. For now, resist the urge to seek shade for your desert garden. Your vegetables, flowers and herbs will require at least six to eight hours of full sun a day. The important factor is the time of day when the garden is exposed.

As you have probably noticed, the angle of the sun as it hits your garden changes with the seasons. In summer, the sun is high overhead; it shines for a longer period of time with a more direct angle. In winter, the sun is lower in the sky; there aren't as many hours of sunlight and its angle is less direct. Think about the sun's path when you decide where to locate your beds. For example, a garden planted close to the north side of a building won't receive direct rays during the winter growing season. South-facing walls are usually the warmest winter locations. A garden planted in front of a west wall will suffer from extreme heat and intense reflected light. Against an east-facing wall, a summer garden will have protection from afternoon sun and light reflection.

Ideal lighting conditions change with the season. A full day of sun in the winter, when days are shorter and cooler, is ideal for vegetables and flowering plants. Cool-weather crops will continue to do well into the spring but will require some shade in the hot afternoon when the weather really begins to heat up. (See "Two Growing Seasons" in Chapter 7 and "Planting Calendars" in Appendix C for more information about cool- and warm-weather crops.) Afternoon shade in the heat of the summer is needed by most crops, some of which can be provided by tall plants like corn and sunflowers or shade cloth stretched on a temporary or permanent structure. You can also accept the reality of heat-stressed plants and wait patiently until the fall brings relief.

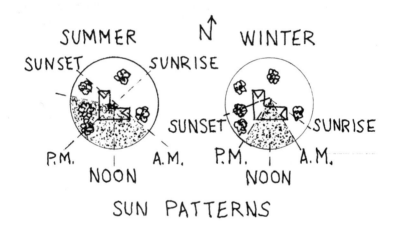

Access to Water

Plants can't survive without water, and the larger the garden, the less likely you'll want to water from buckets and cans. Try to ensure that there is at least one hose bib or faucet within a hose length or two of the garden's farthest corners. If not, extending the reach by burying some PVC pipe to and around the garden to add a few more hose bibs (faucets) is economical, practical (fewer hoses to keep untangled and from mashing other plants) and easy to install with a "T" off the original water system or spigot. Remember to get Schedule 40 PVC pipe, which is the proper thickness to handle water pressure.

A backflow preventer is also an essential part of your watering system. When any water supply is turned off, it can create a suction effect that can reverse water flow from the irrigation system back to the source. This means that anything in your watering system (bacteria, fertilizer, manure) can end up in your drinking water supply traveling via drip irrigation emitters and hoses. Most zoning ordinances require backflow preventers and any hardware, plumbing or irrigation supply shop can give you basic instructions.

Assuming the beds have rims or berms, flooding the area with a hose is probably the easiest method, although it uses more water than some of the other techniques. Also, plants can rot if left in standing water and certain fungal diseases are easily transmitted via wet conditions. If you use a hose, be careful that the force of the water doesn't dislodge seeds or tender transplants or break down earthen berms.

Alternatively, soaker hoses literally "weep" through pores all along the hose, allowing water to soak into the ground at an even, slow rate and lose less to evaporation. Soaker hoses also help prevent disease, as plant leaves don't get wet with each watering. They provide flexibility to move around a bed for different plantings or to different beds within the garden. The disadvantage to soaker hoses is that they may lose water pressure towards the end of the hose if they are too long.

Drip irrigation systems are an efficient and water-saving alternative but may take more time and money to install initially. They are usually less costly in the long term as they save in equipment replacement costs and water use. In arid climates, drip irrigation gets water directly to plant roots with a minimum of loss due to run-off and evaporation. It also helps prevent disease by watering the soil, not the leaves. A typical drip system has main tubes or lines (one-half-inch in diameter) with thinner tubing (often called "spaghetti") running to each plant. An emitter at the end of the spaghetti tubing "drips" water at a slow rate. Emitters can be purchased with different flow rates, such as one gallon per hour.

A variation is to attach laser spaghetti tubing to the main line. Similar to soaker hoses, with tiny holes drilled at equal intervals, the tubing is stretched across the bed, with water seeping at a slow rate. This works well to cover an area of closely planted vegetables or flowers, where numerous tubes with emitters might be less attractive and more costly.

Trenching for a full drip irrigation system with valves and a timer before you establish the beds would be great if you are very confident about your garden layout and have sufficient funds. Hoses are a perfectly acceptable interim solution.

Sprinklers are not recommended as water will hit the plants' leaves, evaporate, and leave salt residues that cause leaf burn. Wet leaves are more susceptible to fungal disease. Also, the deep soil soaking required for good root development generally isn't achieved in the desert with sprinklers.

Level Ground and Soil Drainage

Your garden should be located in a fairly level area. Sloping ground is subject to run-off and erosion, and plant watering needs are difficult to meet. If an area with a slope greater than 20 degrees is your only option, consider adding soil to level the area or building some type of terrace.

Check your soil for drainage by digging a foot-deep hole. Fill it with water and let it drain. Refill it and time how long it takes to drain the second time. The slowest acceptable drainage rate is one inch per hour. If it doesn't drain, you will need to check for and break through a probable hardpan barrier with a pick. There can sometimes be too much of a good thing—even water. Most plants want crumbly-textured, well-draining soil to thrive. Heavy, muddy, hard-packing clay allows little to grow, because plant roots need aeration, too. If, on the other hand, the water drained almost as fast as you poured, you have sandy soil, which will need plentiful amounts of organic matter to help hold moisture. Chapter 2 discusses soil and amendments in more detail.

Raised beds can alleviate some of the problems associated with desert soils, such as extreme compaction and poor drainage. We will explain how to create raised beds in Chapter 5.

Desert Soil

$\mathcal{S}$oil is a complex structure full of living organisms. The more you can learn about your soil's characteristics, the more effective you can be in managing and improving your garden's production.

Soil Texture

Soil texture refers to the relative proportions of sand, silt and clay particles that make up the soil. Sand is the largest particle, silt is the intermediate size and clay is the smallest. Rub some soil with a bit of water between your fingers; sand particles will feel gritty, silt will feel smooth like flour and clay particles will be sticky.

Texture is important because it determines the amount of watering and fertilizing your plants will require. For example, sandy soils drain so fast they don't retain water or nutrients well. Fertilizer leaches, or moves down rapidly, through the soil. Therefore, sand requires more frequent watering and fertilizer applications. However, sand's relatively course structure does provide good aeration for root growth.

On the other end, clay retains water and nutrients well. It will require less frequent watering and fewer applications of fertilizer. However, because the tiny clay particles fit so closely together, poor drainage of water and lack of aeration can cause roots to "drown."

Silt's characteristics fall somewhere in between the other two; silt retains nutrients better than sand and has better drainage than clay. A mixture of clay, silt and sand with generous quantities of organic matter makes an excellent garden soil.

It comes as a surprise to many beginning gardeners that there is little that you can do to significantly change the soil's <u>texture</u>; if you have a clay soil, you will always have a basically clay soil. However, a soil's <u>structure</u> is the more important feature for a garden. The next section tells how to improve soil structure.

Determine Your Soil's Texture

An easy way to determine soil texture is to shake some soil in a jar of water and watch it settle. Sift some soil to remove chunks, pebbles and debris. Put a cup of sifted soil into a straight-sided quart jar. Add one tablespoon each of table salt and laundry detergent. (These act to disperse the negative charge of the clay particles and help eliminate binding between different soil particles.) Add water until almost full. Secure the lid tightly and shake vigorously for five to ten minutes. Put the jar where it won't be disturbed. As the particles settle, sand will reach the bottom first, silt will be next and clay will be the slowest to settle. When the water is clear, all the particles have settled, and you can determine the relative percentages of sand, silt and clay by the thickness of the layers.

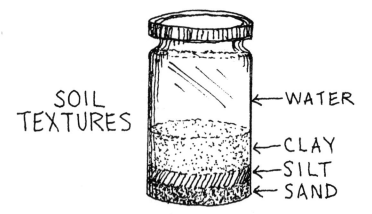

SOIL
TEXTURES

←—WATER

←—CLAY
←—SILT
←— SAND

Soil Structure

Soil structure refers to the arrangement of sand, silt and clay particles in the soil, which determines its permeability and its ability to retain water. For example, soil particles might be clumped together in large chunks that allow water and air to pass through easily, or separated into tiny pieces that fit tightly together like a jigsaw puzzle and prevent water and air from penetrating. As stated earlier, you can't significantly change soil's texture; however, you can improve its structure by adding plentiful amounts of organic matter. Organic matter is the decayed remains of formerly living plants or animals. (See the following list of soil amendments for different types of organic matter.) Adding organic material to clay soils helps improve drainage and aeration; added to sandy soils, organic matter will help retain water and nutrients. Organic matter in all types of soils can improve soil fertility.

Whatever your soil, if you live in the Southwest you should add organic material on a regular basis—at least two or three times per year. Since our soils contain less than one-half of one percent of organic matter, which is continually decomposing into its basic elements, adding organic material is not a one-shot deal but a regular garden maintenance item. Plan on incorporating a three- to six-inch layer of organic matter into the soil before each planting season. This is one of the most important things you can do to improve your garden.

Soil organisms that consume the organic matter and break it down into nutrients for your plants need nitrogen to do their work. For short periods of time, they can actually "rob" the soil of nitrogen that should be feeding your plants. That is why it is important to do one of two things when adding organic matter to your soil:

1. Add organic matter two to three weeks before planting and irrigate thoroughly, allowing the soil organisms to do their work and then release the nitrogen back into the soil for your plants' use. Or,

2. If you can't wait to plant, add a nitrogen source to your organic matter before incorporating it into the soil. (Nitrogen sources are listed below in the "Natural Organic" and "Inorganic" fertilizer tables.)

Organic Soil Amendments

Compost
- Most valuable amendment for desert soils.
- Make it on-site at little or no cost.
- Provides food for beneficial microorganisms and worms.
- Improves sandy soil's ability to retain water and nutrients.
- Improves drainage of clay soil.

Manure
- Use manure only from plant-eating animals, such as cows, sheep, horses, rabbits and chickens. Do not use dog, cat or pet bird manure, which may contain parasites that can spread to humans.
- Should be well-aged (six months) or composted with other materials because its high salt content may burn roots.

Leaves
- Best if composted first. Whole leaves may take a long time to decay and often create a dense mat.
- If no shredder is available, run a lawn mower back and forth over the leaves until shredded.

Pine needles
- Best if composted first. Waxy coating on needles means they can take a long time to decay and prevent the soil from absorbing water.
- Pine needles are acidic and can help lower the high pH (alkalinity) of desert soils.

Cover crops
- Legume crops (peas, beans, alfalfa) are also a good source of nitrogen.
- See "Cover Crops" in Chapter 7 for further information.

Do not use fireplace ashes, which are highly alkaline and will only contribute to the high alkalinity of desert soils.

A constant supply of organic matter in the soil will attract earthworms, those fascinating and hardworking creatures who decompose organic matter and make it available for plants, aerate the soil and leave behind their rich castings, or droppings.

Macronutrients

This is a good time to discuss soil fertility and nutrients. The major nutrients that plants need are nitrogen, phosphorus and potassium, which correspond respectively to the three numbers marked on bags of fertilizer. The numbers represent percentage of contents by weight. For example, a bag of ammonium nitrate (33-0-0) contains 33 percent nitrogen, 0 percent phosphorus and 0 percent potassium. A container of fish meal marked 5-3-3 contains 5 percent nitrogen, 3 percent phosphorus and 3 percent potassium, by weight.

Although the way in which plants use these three nutrients for growth and reproduction is intertwined and extremely complex, it might be helpful for beginning gardeners to think of them in the following manner: nitrogen produces green, lush vegetative growth; phosphorus helps promote root growth and the reproductive cycle (flowers and fruit); and potassium strengthens the plant's hardiness, vigor and disease resistance. Unlike nitrogen, phosphorus does not easily move through the soil with watering. Phosphorus is usually mixed thoroughly into the soil before planting or placed at the bottom of planting holes where it is readily available for uptake by the plant's roots.

Annual flowers and vegetables need nitrogen and phosphorus for quick, single-season bursts of productivity. Perennial herbs need far fewer fertilizer dressings as they will become fairly invasive on their own. Southwestern soils already have plenty of potassium, so if you are purchasing fertilizer, a "zero" for the third number is perfectly acceptable. So is a fertilizer with potassium. Calcium, magnesium and sulfur are other nutrients that plants require. Calcium and sulfur usually aren't added as nutrients because they are incorporated in the form of soil amendments such as gypsum (calcium sulfate) or soil sulfur. These amendments help move sodium beyond the root zones. (See the section on "Sodium in the Soil" below.) Magnesium deficiency is generally not a problem with vegetables, flowers or herbs in our soils.

Micronutrients

In addition to the above macronutrients, there are also micronutrients that are equally important to the health of plants but are needed in much lower quantities. They are boron, chlorine, copper, iron, manganese, molybdenum, and zinc. Compost and other types of organic matter are a good source of micronutrients. Fish emulsion and kelp are other sources. Generally, it is not necessary to apply micronutrients to annual flowers, herbs and vegetables. Check with the Cooperative Extension office for local conditions.

Fertilizers

Organic fertilizers contain carbon; they may be natural or man-made. Natural organic fertilizers are derived from the decayed remains of formerly living things and have had minimal processing, such as bone meal or fish meal. Man-made organic fertilizers, such as urea, are synthetically manufactured from materials containing carbon. When we talk about organic fertilizers in this book, we are referring to the natural organics.

Soil microorganisms will further decompose organic fertilizers, and this slow-release process feeds both the soil and the plants during the growing season. Organic fertilizers help to foster abundant microbial life in the soil. Over time, less nitrogen needs to be added to the soil.

Inorganic or synthetic chemical fertilizers are man-made and contain no organic (carbon) elements. They are made from mineral salts. They are usually more highly concentrated and less expensive than organic fertilizers. Inorganic products generally contain only nitrogen, phosphorus and potassium so they don't have some of the indirect benefits, such as micronutrients or organic matter, that organic products can have. Because they are highly concentrated, inorganic fertilizers can burn the plant if too much is used or it is placed too close to the roots.

How quickly nutrients are available to plants is largely determined by their solubility in water. If the fertilizer is not water soluble, then the plants can't absorb it immediately. It must first be consumed by soil microorganisms and then released. Inorganic fertilizers are often in a form that is released and absorbed more quickly by the plants than are organic fertilizers. There are also slow-release inorganic fertilizers. They are in a pellet form with a coating that gradually decomposes and releases the fertilizer to the plant. Slow-release fertilizers tend to be more expensive than other types.

Choosing a Fertilizer

Which should you use? Plants do not differentiate between an organic or inorganic nutrient. The form that the nutrient takes when it is absorbed by the plants' roots is the same whether it was derived from a natural or a synthetic source. But fertilizers are more than just nutrient carriers, and they impact more than just the plants. The misuse of fertilizers can kill microorganisms, alter soil characteristics, pollute water supplies and may even affect pest and disease resistance.

Some people believe that the "ecological profile" of a fertilizer is more important than whether it was dug from the ground or "produced" in some way. Not all "natural products" are healthy (e.g., grass clippings from a lawn that has been heavily treated with herbicides and pesticides); and not all synthetic products are bad for the environment. For example, elemental sulfur, which can help control plant diseases and neutralize soil alkalinity, may be naturally mined or scrubbed from industrial smoke stacks. Distinguishing between sulfur obtained from these two different sources is difficult. Using the waste-product from the smoke stacks promotes clean-air controls and makes them more economically feasible. This may be a more environmentally sound practice than mining.

As you can see, there are many variables to consider when selecting a fertilizer. Examine the accompanying charts for some of the pros and cons of each type. As you continue to add organic material to the soil over the years and become more familiar with the nutritional needs of plants, you may discover that you do not need to rely on the quick bursts of elements provided by synthetic fertilizers. Appendix A lists books on organic gardening if you want further information.

Questions To Ask When Choosing A Fertilizer

It is probably not possible to answer all of these questions for each fertilizer. However, it is a good place to start to consider the many choices available and the possible long-term consequences.

1. How quickly will the nutrients be absorbed by the plants?
2. What effects will it have on plant growth and health?
3. What is its cost?
4. Is it convenient to use?
5. What will it do to, or for, soil organisms?
6. Can it lead to air or water pollution?
7. Does its mining, manufacture or transport harm the environment?
8. How energy intensive is it to produce?
9. Does it recycle an existing organic waste product?
10. Is there an alternative that may be more environmentally benign?

Natural Organic Fertilizers

Type	Primary element	N-P-K ratio
Alfalfa meal	Nitrogen	5-1-2
Blood meal	Nitrogen	14-0-0
Coffee grounds	Nitrogen	7-2-2
Cottonseed meal	Nitrogen	6-2-1
Fish emulsion	Nitrogen	5-2-2
Seabird guano	Nitrogen	1-12-0.5
Bone meal	Phosphorus*	1-11-0
Rock phosphate	Phosphorus*	0-3-0
Greensand	Potassium	0-0-7
Seaweed/kelp	Potassium	1-0.5-2.5
Compost	varies	0.5-0.5-0.5 to 4-4-4

N-P-K analysis can vary considerably.
*These decompose and release phosphorus very slowly in alkaline soils. A little soil sulfur added with it can speed up the process.

Advantages
- Slower to leach from soil; fewer applications required.
- Encourages beneficial soil organisms and worms.
- Improves soil structure, including aeration and moisture-holding capacity.
- Little or no salt build up.
- Difficult to overfertilize and burn plants.
- Most contain micronutrients.
- Compost recycles yard waste rather than sending it to landfills.

Disadvantages
- Takes longer to decompose and allow nutrients to be available to plants.
- May need to be combined with other types to create a complete fertilizer.
- Analysis of NPK ratio can vary; ratio is usually low.
- Usually not as concentrated as synthetic fertilizers.
- Cost per pound of nutrients is higher.

Inorganic Fertilizers

Type	Primary element	N-P-K ratio
Ammonium nitrate	Nitrogen	33-0-0
Ammonium sulfate	Nitrogen	21-0-0
Ammonium phosphate	Phosphorus	16-20-0
Triple super phosphate	Phosphorus	0-45-0

Advantages
- Nutrients are more quickly available to plants than with organic fertilizers.
- Higher or more concentrated nutrient levels.
- Cost per pound of nutrients is often lower.

Disadvantages
- Nitrogen generally leaches through the soil fairly quickly, so requires more frequent applications.
- Overfertilizing may burn plants.
- No beneficial impact to the soil's structure.
- Do not provide organic matter, which is extremely important for soil fertility and workability.
- Many are easily volatilized (lost to the air) if not immediately watered in.

Soil pH

Soil pH is a measure of the soil's level of acidity or alkalinity on a scale from 0–14. Readings below a neutral 7 are acidic; those above are alkaline. Southwestern desert soils generally register between 7.5 and 8.5. Unlike much of the rest of the nation, we do not add lime to our soils, which would cause increased alkalinity.

A soil's pH level influences plant growth by affecting the availability of nutrients and the concentration of minerals. Nutrients are more available to the plants in the neutral range. In alkaline soils, micronutrients such as iron, zinc, copper and manganese can become chemically "tied up" and thus unavailable for plant use. The addition of organic matter, which puts acidic compounds in the soil, can improve pH on a temporary and localized basis. This adjustment to the pH makes minerals like iron more available to, or easily absorbed by, the plants.

Sodium in the Soil

Clay soils have a tendency to attract and hold sodium (in addition to other nutrients), and our limited rainfall does not usually leach sodium from the soil. Our water contains sodium, and after we irrigate, evaporation will tend to leave it and other salts on the soil surface. Shallow and frequent watering practices, which may moisten only the top few inches of soil, add more salt to the soil surface. (See Chapter 8 for a discussion of correct watering practices.) As sodium accumulates, it disperses the clay particles and impedes water penetration through the soil. To remedy the situation, apply gypsum or soil sulfur and water deeply (12–24"). Calcium in the gypsum will cause sodium in the soil to be leached beyond the root zone. Soil sulfur will accomplish the same result through a different set of chemical reactions in the soil. Gypsum and soil sulfur are considered to be inorganic soil amendments because they contain no carbon.

As with the addition of organic matter, this is not a permanent solution and should be repeated yearly. Incorporating one of these products into the soil during bed preparation is easiest. Follow package directions to determine how much to apply.

Inorganic Soil Amendments

Gypsum (calcium sulfate)
- Improves the structure of clay soils and thus helps improve drainage.

Soil sulfur
- Improves the structure of clay soils and thus helps improve drainage.
- A naturally occurring mineral that can, on a limited basis, lower soil pH and make some nutrients more available to plants.
- Some organic gardeners believe that soil sulfur is detrimental to earthworms, particularly if it is not well mixed into the soil.
- Sulfur is not recommended for soils that will be growing onions, as it makes them more pungent.

Removing Bermudagrass

*B*efore you can add amendments, your plot needs to be cleared of existing vegetation and debris, and the soil tilled. If your new garden is now a barren spot where there are few plants to remove, you won't need this information, although you should ask yourself why nothing is growing there!

Many of you will be facing an array of weeds that can be removed by an herbicide or by tilling and raking. But if your lot also contains Bermudagrass or nutsedge (also called nutgrass), this element of site development will take more time. Other perennial weeds that can be difficult to remove include Johnsongrass, blueweed, bindweed, puncturevine and tumbleweed. If you make the effort to remove these now, it will pay off handsomely later.

Chemical Method of Removal

Although you will not be an organic gardener in the strict sense of the term, you may still want to use one chemical, at least initially, to clear your garden plot of weeds. The ingredient called glyphosate (sold under different trade names) is used to reduce the tenacious growth of Bermudagrass and nutsedge. Glyphosate is a "systemic," meaning that it is sprayed directly on the plant, which absorbs and distributes it throughout its system. Eventually it kills the entire plant, including the growth areas in the roots, rhizomes and stolons. You should not spray glyphosate on desirable plants. Glyphosate is not active in our soils, so there should be no carryover to new plants.

For best results, glyphosate needs to be applied when the vegetation is growing vigorously, which means warm weather (summer) application. Water the weed to promote vigorous growth;

when it is thriving, spray it with glyphosate. Yes, it's true—you must first stimulate the growth of weeds in order to kill them. The spray is absorbed through the green leaves, so have at least a few inches of growth; don't crop the grass down to the ground. Apply exactly as directed on the container's label, wait about two weeks by which time all the plants should be brown, irrigate well and reapply the glyphosate when any regrowth reaches several inches in height. Bermuda can be eliminated after two thorough applications; several more applications may be required for nutsedge. (In fact, we consider nutsedge so difficult that, given a choice between two locations with and without this weed, we would take the latter.) Carefully remove any regrowth after establishing the garden.

Organic Method of Removal

Bermuda lawns can be removed by digging out the top 6 to 12 inches of grass and painstakingly removing the stolons (or disposing of this entire layer including soil). Bermudagrass is tenacious, and some Master Gardeners recommend digging even deeper to remove stubborn growth. How far you dig may depend upon the size of your rototiller, available labor and examination of your soil for growth. One thing is certain: you won't get it all the first time.

Another organic alternative is to cover the areas of undesirable growth with clear plastic for one season (March through October). Do not stretch the plastic too tightly or some plants may grow through. If fresh manure is available, a layer under the plastic will help heat up the area. Intense heat and lack of moisture will kill much of the Bermuda, but stolons below 12 inches or so will continue to grow to the surface. Applying thick layers of mulch to paths and beds and pulling out Bermuda as soon as it appears will make it more difficult for it to gain control.

4

Tips for Designing the Garden

We cannot overemphasize the importance of planting only as large a garden as you can comfortably maintain. Beginning gardeners can sometimes overplant and become overwhelmed with the weeding and watering needs. A small but beautifully maintained set of beds is of much greater value than a large, unkempt plot. Monitor your successes and failures and expand your garden as your confidence and level of experience build.

An ample number of pathways is critical. Although they mean extra work during site preparation, they will provide lots of angles from which to view and work plots. It's important to stay out of the beds to minimize soil compaction and plant destruction. Use sheets of newspaper or a weed barrier product covered with several inches of mulch, dried grass, wood chips or crushed stone to minimize the weeds.

Invest some time on mapping out your garden. The sun's path and your bed's orientation (North-South or East-West) will influence crop placement. You won't want a tall crop to completely shade a low-growing vegetable for the entire day. Locate tall plants so they will provide shade during summer afternoons. (See Chapter 1 for a diagram of the sun's path.) Allow yourself to think in terms of plant clusters or "square foot gardening" for your garden's design.

Square Foot Gardening

Mel Bartholomew developed square foot gardening, which is a method of planting in adjacent squares rather than in traditional long rows. Each square is 12 inches by 12 inches, thus the name, "square foot gardening." Bartholomew recommends that these one-foot squares be grouped into larger 4-foot by 4-foot blocks of 16 total squares (four down and four across), each containing a different vegetable, flower or herb. If gardening with children or anyone who might have difficulty reaching across the beds, we recommend modifying this to 3-foot by 3-foot blocks with nine total squares. This block allows easy access to each square without stepping on the soil. These blocks become permanent planting beds that are never compacted by foot traffic, allowing the soil to retain its light, crumbly quality.

The number of seeds sowed per square depends upon the variety, how much space the mature plant will require and the space needed between plants. For example, a large plant such as a pepper would be set alone in the middle of a square. Another square could accommodate 12 smaller plants, such as carrots or scallions, that require only three inches of growing room. Even larger plants, such as eggplants or tomatoes, might need two to four squares. Plants that sprawl over a large area, such as zucchini or cucumbers, can be trained to grow vertically on sturdy supports.

Because there is no wasted space between long rows, advocates of square foot gardening claim the same harvests as do gardeners using the row method, but use only 20 percent of the total space. This translates into considerable dollar savings in water, soil amendments, fertilizer and labor. Bartholomew's book detailing the specifics of square foot gardening, including spacing for plants and basic layouts, is listed in Appendix A.

SQUARE FOOT
GARDEN
3' X 3'

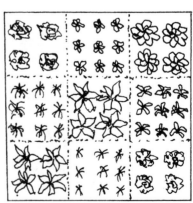

Preparing the Soil

*I*t is usually helpful to soak the garden area several days before digging to soften the soil. However, do not begin to till or dig before the soil has dried enough to crumble in your hands. If you squeeze some soil in your hand and it forms a ball, it's too wet to work. Or, if soil sticks to your shovel, it is still too wet to work. **NOTE: You can permanently damage the soil structure by working it when it is still too wet.**

To break up and aerate compacted soil, begin by rototilling or digging deeply, at least 12–18 inches. In very hard soils, you may even need a pick. Don't relocate the garden because you think you hit caliche. Although caliche exists throughout the Southwest, there are many areas that just suffer from extremely hard-packed soil. Find someone knowledgeable to examine the area. A series of soakings, partial dryings and pickings, with additions of organic material, should eventually yield workable soil.

Work amendments into the top 10 inches of soil. You may choose to keep costs down by amending only the planting areas, not the pathways. Or it may simply be easier to cover the whole plot, particularly if you do not plan for stationary beds.

To open up heavy clay, increase water retention in sandy soils, and to improve aeration and fertility for all soils, add generous amounts of organic matter, up to 1/3 by volume (refer to the list of organic amendments in Chapter 2). If you are adding other fertilizers (especially phosphorus, which needs to be placed in the root zone), apply them at this time following the instructions on the container. Sulfur should be used in almost any flower or vegetable bed, with the exception of onions which become overly pungent. Gypsum can be supplemented for sodium control if you 1) have heavy clay soil, and 2) the soil crusts, cracks or blocks when dry.

Another thorough irrigation, with water penetrating at least two feet, will leach harmful salts from the future root zone in the soil. (Poke a rod or stick into the ground to measure moisture depth.) This is important particularly if you have used certain saltier manures (horse and chicken). Let the soil "simmer" for a few weeks before planting. This will allow for further amendment decomposition and drying out of the soil. A final turning and raking before planting day is a good idea. If you are not using a drip irrigation system and have level beds, create a shallow basin using a berm or small dike of dirt around the edge to allow for flood irrigation and salt accumulation on this lip.

Raised Beds

A raised bed is simply soil that is improved and built up, or raised, above ground level. The advantages of raised beds are improved drainage and no compaction from foot traffic. Over time, it is usually easier to improve soil structure and fertility in the confines of a raised bed. Raised beds make gardening possible for those who are physically challenged or who can not easily bend or kneel. Interesting geometric patterns can be created with raised beds as well as different levels or tiers.

Many gardeners prefer to place borders around raised beds to prevent erosion from wind, watering and working the soil. Lumber, bricks, cement blocks and stones can be used as borders. Be sure to use lumber that has not been chemically treated so chemicals won't leach into your soil over time.

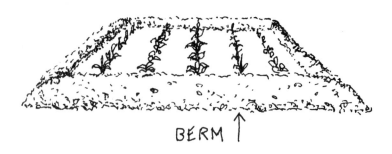

BERM ↑

If borders are not available, the soil can be raked and the beds "remade" before each planting. Borders can be added at a later time.

It is a good idea to loosen the soil and work it as described above to improve drainage and root penetration. Then build up a layer of soil approximately 8–12 inches deep, mixing soil from your garden with generous amounts of organic matter. Each planting season, continue to build your soil by adding organic matter and soil amendments.

The next section describes an alternative method of building raised beds over time.

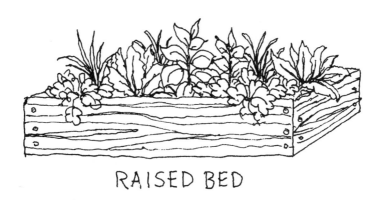

RAISED BED

Permaculture

The concept of permaculture was developed by Australian Bill Mollison over 20 years ago after observing native cultures and natural ecosystems. Permaculture is a contraction of "permanent agriculture" and "permanent culture." Its guiding principle is to observe nature and then mimic it, thus lessening our impact on the earth.

Permaculture encompasses different techniques and materials for different climates. A complete discussion of all its principles is beyond the scope of this book, but we have included a permaculture method for building good soil without the preliminary heavy digging required with traditional soil preparation. To learn more about permaculture, check the listings in Appendix A.

Soil Preparation

Start with the original layer of soil, undisturbed. Sprinkle blood meal or cottonseed meal at the rates indicated on the container over the entire area. Spread about six inches of manure on top of the meal. Water this layer until just moist throughout. The meal and manure are organic nitrogen sources, which will generate heat to kill weed seeds and disease pathogens. It's best to use manure that has aged for two or three months. If only fresh manure is available, continue with the layering process, but let it sit for two months or so before planting. Fresh, or "hot," manure can "burn" tender plant roots.

Next, layer one-quarter-inch of newspaper or cardboard on top of the manure. Use rocks or bricks to prevent them from blowing around as you spread them on the ground. Moisten this layer thoroughly.

Finally, layer six inches of straw on top. Water this layer until moist. If the manure is aged, you are ready to plant!

Planting

Push aside an opening (about the size of your fist) in the straw. Poke a hole through the layer of newspaper or cardboard so that plant roots will be able to grow. Fill the opening with soil from your garden. This soil will be loaded with microorganisms that will help decompose the organic layers. Plant seeds or transplants.

This method mimics what happens on a forest floor—leaves and pine needles pile up, animals leave droppings, rain falls. If you scoop below that top layer of leaves, you will probably find a rich, dark crumbly soil. This is what you are trying to achieve in your garden. Over time, the straw and manure will decompose and build a layer of rich organic matter.

For the next planting season, you can repeat the layering process or plant directly into the decomposed layer. If you are planting during the hot summer months, you will need to plant deeper to prevent the column of dirt from drying out. You may need to dig below the newspaper layer into the decomposing manure to plant. Small seeds may have difficulty germinating if the straw drifts over and covers them.

The obvious advantage to this method is that you can begin planting immediately without any heavy digging. This is particularly helpful if you don't have access to rototillers or strong labor. Children can easily handle this method of building good soil and learn about nature's recycling process at the same time.

Maricopa County Master Gardeners tried this permaculture method in their Demonstration Garden and were pleased with the results. Remember: there are many ways to garden! Many life-long gardeners enjoy the challenge of trying something different, whether it is a new seed variety, soil preparation method or "secret" fertilizer recipe. Enjoy experimenting and finding what works best for you.

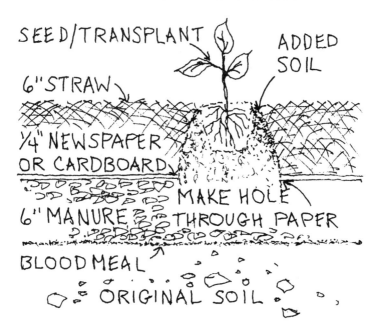

INSTANT GARDEN

SEED/TRANSPLANT — ADDED SOIL

6" STRAW

¼" NEWSPAPER OR CARDBOARD

6" MANURE — MAKE HOLE THROUGH PAPER

BLOOD MEAL

ORIGINAL SOIL

6

Making Compost

*F*inished compost is dark, crumbly organic matter that has a fresh, earthy smell. There's no real mystery to making compost. It's a natural process of decomposition that goes on all around us as nature's recycling system. A properly created compost pile doesn't smell or attract rodents and flies. This chapter contains some basic techniques that you can use to create compost for your garden. If you become fascinated by the process, as many gardeners do, there are several books listed in the references that provide more detail.

Compost is an excellent soil amendment. Healthy plants need healthy soil to thrive and adding compost is probably the best thing you can do to improve your soil's fertility and workability. Compost improves drainage and aeration in clay soils; it helps to retain water and nutrients in sandy soils. It provides food for earthworms and a multitude of microorganisms that break down organic matter, making nutrients available to your plants.

In addition, about one-fourth of all refuse sent to the landfills consists of landscape debris and yard waste. Composting this material saves the time and expense of bagging and hauling it away and reduces the amount of refuse sent to landfills. Interestingly, this organic matter doesn't decompose quickly in the landfills, since two ingredients required for the process—water and air circulation—aren't readily available.

Compost Ingredients

There are four basic ingredients required to make compost: carbon, nitrogen, water and oxygen.

Carbon is found in "brown" matter such as dried leaves, straw, shredded paper towels, cardboard and newspaper, corn stalks, woody yard trimmings, pine needles and sawdust. Nitrogen is contained in "green" matter such as grass clippings, fresh garden trimmings, weeds before they go to seed, kitchen scraps (no meats, dairy or oils) and manure from plant-eating barnyard animals.

In reality, all organic matter contains some ratio of carbon and nitrogen. For example, sawdust can have a ratio of 500:1, or 500 parts carbon to 1 part nitrogen. Grass clippings have a ratio of 20:1, or 20 parts carbon to 1 part nitrogen. We label these materials as carbon-rich or nitrogen-rich based upon their average ratios (see table on next page).

The "ideal" compost pile contains a carbon to nitrogen mix of 30:1. Most of the organisms decomposing the pile prefer more carbon (which they use for energy) than nitrogen (which is used to build their bodies and reproduce). Try to balance the materials in your compost pile accordingly. For example, you can use sawdust (extremely high in carbon) sparingly if well incorporated with plenty of nitrogen-rich materials. However, if you fill a bin full of sawdust and sprinkle a few grass clippings over the top, in a few years you'll still have a bin full of sawdust.

Don't let the carbon to nitrogen ratios scare you away—you don't need a calculator to compost. If you use a mix of about equal parts carbon-rich and nitrogen-rich materials (e.g., two wheelbarrows of crushed, dry leaves plus two wheelbarrows of grass clippings) or two parts carbon to one part nitrogen, you'll be off to a good start—as long as you don't use too much of the very high carbon materials, such as sawdust, woody brush and newspaper. The more variety in your materials, the better. And the smaller the pieces, the faster the decomposition, so it pays to chop and shred the material as much as possible.

Water and oxygen are also essential for the organisms to do their work. Add water to the pile when it's created and when it's turned. Moisture is also present in some of the green materials, such as grass clippings. If the pile dries out or isn't turned to provide aeration, the composting process will slow down dramatically as the bacteria die off. Think of composting as providing a friendly environment in which the microorganisms can live while they decompose organic matter for your personal use.

Carbon to Nitrogen Ratios

Carbon (browns)	Carbon : Nitrogen
Sawdust	200-500 : 1
Woody landscape prunings	300 : 1
Newspaper	150-200 : 1
Straw	50-80 : 1
Corn stalks	50-60 : 1
Dry leaves	40-80 : 1
Dry hay	40 : 1

Nitrogen (greens)	
Fresh hay	10-25 : 1
Kitchen scraps	15-25 : 1
Leafy prunings and leftover crops	20-25 : 1
Grass clippings	20-25 : 1
Rotted manures	20-25 : 1
Chicken manure	10 : 1

Items to avoid

- Meats, bones, dairy, oils, greases. May attract pests and become rancid.
- Cat, dog, pet bird manure. Can contain pathogens.
- Weed seeds, weed runners (e.g., Bermudagrass) or diseased plants. Best to avoid if you can't maintain temperatures of 140-150 degrees Fahrenheit as this trio can easily survive in low-temperature piles.
- Glossy magazine paper and newspaper inserts. Coated with a clay that resists water and decomposition. May contain heavy metals.
- Fireplace ashes. Extremely alkaline. Most desert soils are already alkaline.

Constructing a pile

Piles can be as simple as a heap in an out-of-the-way spot in your backyard. A shaded pile will not dry out as fast as one in the sun. For optimum decomposition, a pile should be at least 3 feet by 3 feet by 3 feet, or 1 cubic yard in size. This allows enough mass for a pile to "heat up" and insulate itself. Piles larger than 5 feet cubed don't allow enough air to reach the center.

If you prefer, you can build or buy an enclosure for the compost. Some inexpensive types can be made from wire mesh or shipping pallets. Also many cities offer free or inexpensive compost bins made from recycled garbage containers.

You can construct the pile in about 2- to 12-inch layers, or you can mix it all together like a salad. Many experienced composters think that mixing the ingredients at the beginning helps decomposition get off to a fast start. Alternate green with the brown and thoroughly moisten with a garden hose as you go. A spray gun on the hose is very helpful. All the material should feel similar to a moist sponge. Constructing the pile and then trying to soak it all from the top down doesn't work, as the water runs to the bottom of the pile in channels. If possible, add a shovelful or two of soil or finished compost, which adds millions of bacteria to begin the decomposing process.

If all conditions are optimum—water, oxygen, carbon and nitrogen, small pieces, in one cubic yard—the bacteria will start decomposing the organic matter in a frenzy. Heat energy is released from the decomposition process. The pile's heat does not come from the sun. A hot pile can reach 140-160 degrees Fahrenheit in just two or three days. As the water and air are used up, the pile's temperature will start to drop. To reactivate the pile, turn it with a pitchfork to aerate and add needed moisture. If temperatures don't rise again and the pile is "young," you might need to add more nitrogen materials. Temperatures will decrease as the pile "matures" and transforms into finished compost.

You can buy a compost thermometer that's about 18 inches long from some nurseries and garden catalogs. Monitoring the temperature is important if you want to manage the pile to produce compost quickly.

If you consistently turn and moisten the pile as its temperature begins to drop, you will maintain a hot pile and will have compost in one to three months. If you don't have time to monitor or work the pile, composting will continue, but at a much slower rate. An unmanaged pile may take six or more months before its compost is ready to use.

What's Wrong with the Compost Pile?

Problem	Cause	Solution
Slow decomposition	Lack of nitrogen	Add "greens"
	Poor aeration	Turn pile*
	Too dry	Add water while turning pile
	Pile too small**	Add to pile
Ammonia smell	Too much nitrogen	Add high-carbon materials; remix to add oxygen
Rotten smell	Too much water	Add dry carbon materials; remix
Pile attracts flies/pests	Food scraps too close to surface	Bury scraps in center of pile; cover with 4-6" of compost
Pile contains grubs, worms and other large insects	Nature at work!	Do nothing; they are composters working for you!

*Large pieces of stems and corn stalks provide air pockets, but won't compost quickly. When compost is ready, take out larger pieces and put in a new pile.

**Minimum pile size for fast decomposition is 1 cubic yard.

7

Planting and Tending

*B*uilding good soil can be satisfying, but now the fun really begins. At times it may seem that we've turned upside down some of the gardening practices you may have learned in another area of the country. But if you follow these few basic guidelines for desert gardening, you'll be harvesting buckets of produce and armloads of flowers in no time!

Seeds

Choose varieties that are known to do well in the desert. Give preference to disease- and pest-resistant selections. This information can be found as letters at the end of the species name in the catalog description or on the seed packet. For example, "Celebrity VFNT" is a tomato that is resistant to Verticillium, Fusarium, Nematodes and Tobacco Mosaic, all problems that can strike tomatoes. If you have limited space, use dwarf varieties. In general, select varieties with shorter growing cycles to help deal with the relatively short cool- and warm-weather growing seasons in the desert. Plants with short growing cycles often have "Early" in their name. Many catalogs contain charts with this type of information so that you can compare plant attributes. If this seems confusing, consult your County Cooperative Extension office, local garden clubs, community garden newsletters, garden columns in local periodicals, nurseries and seed companies in the Southwest. They can recommend varieties that do well in your area.

Follow seed package instructions for row and plant spacing or follow the square foot gardening guide. Consider halving the recommended planting depth since our soil is usually heavier. Lacking seed instructions, a rule of thumb is a depth of two to three times the seed diameter. If you have a heavy clay soil that could form a crust over young germinating seeds, lightly cover the seeds with sand or mulch. (The more you improve the soil with organic matter over time, the less likely you will need to do this.) Gently water seeds to retain moist, not muddy, soil. Commence deep watering practices (see Chapter 8) when plants emerge.

As to planting dates, desert gardening references or Cooperative Extension publications will provide better information than seed packages or books written for other climates. If plants don't sprout within the expected time frame, replant immediately. Check your seed packs for dates. It's not that old seed won't grow, but the percentage that will germinate starts to fall as the seed ages.

Some seeds are treated with chemicals to prevent seedling diseases. Treated seeds are usually colored. Wash hands thoroughly after handling treated seeds.

Transplants

When buying transplants, select healthy, pest-free, mid-sized plants. Do not buy plants too large for the container as the plant may be root-bound. Leave behind the spindly, yellowed or spotted starters. You can start your own transplants from seed in bright indoor light (16 hours/day) or in a greenhouse about six to eight weeks before planting time. Before transplanting, "harden them off," which is the process of acclimating the plants to outdoor weather conditions. Set the plants out for an hour or two daily and gradually increase their length of exposure over one or two weeks.

Transplant on cloudy days or in the evenings if possible to reduce the possibility of moisture stress. Water the plants the day before or several hours before transplanting to prevent sudden wilting when removed from the containers. Keep the root ball intact and handle plants carefully. If the roots have circled the container (called girdling), loosen the ends of the roots gently with your fingers. If necessary, draw a pointed instrument such as a nail or pencil down the side of the root ball or cut the roots as a last resort.

Seedlings should be transplanted at the same level in the soil as they were in their containers. The ground around them should be level. Don't plant them up on little hills or in sunken depressions. The hills carry water away from the plant and may erode, exposing the roots. Depressions will collect water and increase the chances of waterborne diseases or stem rot. Salts will also accumulate. (Tomatoes are an exception to this rule. See Chapter 11 for tips on planting tomatoes.)

Be sure to soak the ground well immediately after transplanting. Protection from sun and wind for a few days is helpful.

Two Growing Seasons

Desert newcomers are pleasantly surprised to learn that we have two distinct growing seasons—a warm season and a cool season—in which different plants will thrive. Warm-season annuals are typically planted from March through September and grow through summer and fall until killed by the first frost, usually around late November. Cool-season plants are started from approximately September through November to establish good root systems before temperatures drop. They will grow and bloom through the winter and spring until warm weather sets in around April.

The Planting Calendars provide a range of dates that offer a high probability of success. Use them as a guideline and adjust as necessary. Yearly weather conditions can vary considerably and the desert contains a myriad of microclimates—areas with specific conditions due to such factors as elevation or sun exposure.

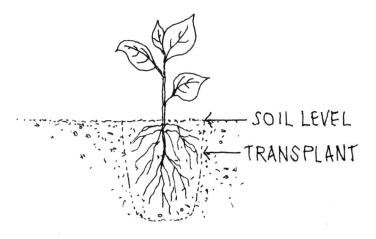

SOIL LEVEL

TRANSPLANT

Mulch

When your plants are up, mulch, mulch, mulch. Mulching is covering the soil with some type of material, organic or inorganic. We favor organic matter because it minimizes water evaporation, keeps the soil from baking in the hot sun, provides a protective barrier against weeds and eventually enriches the soil when you turn it under or it breaks down. Some temporary nitrogen depletion may occur, but this is minimal. Remove the mulch during cooler months (January–March), if quick spring crop germination requires warm soil. You could even heat the soil by covering it with clear plastic.

Types of Organic Mulches

compost	leaves	straw
grass clippings	hay	cottonseed hulls
pine needles	wood chips	sawdust

Materials that decompose more slowly and are high in carbon (wood chips, sawdust) temporarily rob nitrogen from the soil. They are better left to pathways where the soil can still receive long-term conditioning.

Don't use anything as mulch that could break down and be harmful to your plants, such as sawdust from chemically treated lumber.

Weeds

Control the weeds in the garden, which can compete with your plants for water, sun and nutrients. But don't let this year-round task control you. Mulching is a great way to discourage unwanted plants by providing a barrier between stray weed seeds and the soil. Weeds can provide food and shelter for insect pests such as cutworms or whiteflies. Although scientists have done some research on weeds serving as food and shelter for beneficial insects, such as lady beetles, the results are not conclusive.

Be forewarned: most weeds reseed prolifically, so if you don't remove them before they flower and go to seed, you will have a huge new crop next year. Pull the weeds <u>before</u> they go to seed and put them in your compost pile. Use your hands or tools, but you shouldn't have to use chemicals for weed control.

Thinning

There should be limited need to thin if seeds have been correctly spaced, but we don't always sow uniformly. Many gardeners hate the thought of pulling up seedlings, but fewer, well-spaced plants will actually produce more harvest, not less. Thinning should be started about two weeks after sprouts appear.

Thin by cutting seedlings at ground level with scissors. There is less chance of disturbing adjacent plant roots.

Fertilizing

If you have prepared your soil well at the beginning of the growing season, you may not need to bother with midseason fertilization. It depends on the needs of your plants and the fertility of your soil. Examine your plants for any of the symptoms listed in Appendix B, "Diagnosing Plant Problems." If you determine the need for an extra "boost," there are several methods for applying fertilizer mid-season. Always apply fertilizer according to the container's instructions.

Dilute foliar sprays are mixed with water and sprayed directly on the plant, which absorbs the nutrients through its leaves.

More concentrated water-soluble fertilizers are mixed with water and applied to the soil around the plant. Take care not to splash on the plant itself.

Alternatively, fertilizer can be dug into the soil about four inches to the side of your plants and worked to a depth of three inches. If the fertilizer is applied more closely, you will risk burning the roots.

Summer Gardening

Maintaining the garden through the summer can be a challenge. It may be most helpful to you and the garden to consider this a time of much-needed rest for, and rejuvenation of, the soil. Unlike a temperate climate garden that lies fallow under a bed of leaves in the winter, your garden in the desert will never "get a break" unless you use some summers for periods of inactivity. This is a good time to solarize the soil if you have nematode, disease or weed problems or to plant a cover crop to enrich the soil before fall planting resumes.

Solarization

Solarization can be thought of as pasteurizing the soil through trapped solar radiation. Cultivate manure into the soil, water well (we're talking steam heat in this process), cover loosely with clear, heavy plastic, about 1–2 millimeters thick, and bury the edges. A minimum of six weeks of solarization is required for the extreme heat to reach the pathogens and weed seeds at lower soil depths.

Cover Crops

Feeding the soil with a cover crop is easy. A cover crop is simply homegrown organic matter that is planted directly into the soil that you want to improve. In the summer, alfalfa, buckwheat, soybeans or sorghum can be a good cover crop. You must turn the crops under (till them into the ground) before the reproductive (flower) stage so that the plants do not start using up the nitrogen they have just stored in their root systems and which you want to keep in the soil. When turned under young, a cover-cropped garden can be recultivated and seeded in two or three weeks.

8

Effective Watering in the Desert

*Y*ou might prefer an easily communicated time schedule of watering frequencies, but the reality is that site drainage, soil structure, temperature, sun and wind exposure and the time of year are all variables of this critical maintenance task. Excessive fluctuation in soil moisture can negatively impact plants. It's even possible to overirrigate in the desert! Observation of your plants and soil is the only way to water wisely.

Frequent, gentle waterings are needed to germinate seeds. Maintain moist (not wet) soil in the top two to three inches, which also helps prevent a surface "crust" from forming, allowing seedlings to more easily emerge. After your sprouts emerge, waterings become less frequent but deeper to match the enlarging root zone and to leach, or move, salts below the root zone. Your goal is to keep at least the top foot moist. Use a soil probe to measure periodically in the early morning. (A soil probe can be any long, thin object that you can thrust into the soil, such as a screwdriver or ruler. If the probe moves easily, the soil is moist. Where the probe stops, the soil is dry.) Morning is the best time to irrigate, to prevent the growth or spread of waterborne disease or pests. If the soil is dry down to one inch, then water the garden.

After seedlings are established, allow the soil to just barely dry out between slow, deep waterings. This encourages strong root development and allows for aeration in the soil. Remember, it is possible to drown or rot your plants if you overwater clay soil; roots also need oxygen.

In general, larger plants will use more water than smaller ones. Plants with deep roots are watered less often than shallow-rooted ones. More water is needed during summer heat and drying winds. Clay and silt soils retain water longer than sandy soil.

Wilt is often a sign of water deprivation, meaning the soil has an inadequte amount of moisture for plants to draw upon. However, take care when examining large, leafy plants such as squash, melons and sweet potatoes which may suffer from heat stress during summer afternoons. During heat stress, there is adequate moisture in the soil, but the transpiration (moisture loss) rate from the plant's leaves exceeds the rate of water absorption by the roots. The foliage wilts in the hot afternoon, but can recover during the cooler evening hours if adequate soil moisture is present. If plants recover the following morning and the soil seems moist based on the above rule, hold the water. Adding more water can actually promote root rot. Learn to tolerate summer heat stress in your garden. Most plants will not look their finest in August, but if you allow the plants to develop some coping capacity you will minimize your watering chores. You might try providing afternoon shade for heat-stressed plants.

Water the soil, not the plants. Showering foliage will have negligible soil impact and increases the chance of vegetative salt burn or the spread of fungal disease.

9

Managing Insects

Insects are a fact of life in an outdoor garden. They are needed for pollination of many plants; numerous fruits and vegetables couldn't develop without the friendly aid of busy bees (unless you want to hand pollinate rows of vegetables!). In fact, one third of the food we eat is the direct result of pollination by insects. Some insects are called beneficials, because they eat or parasitize harmful insects that are damaging our plants. Even "bad bugs" are doing nature's work of breaking down plant tissue into reusable elements. However, they work on their timetable, not ours!

Everybody's favorite beneficial is the lady beetle (sometimes called lady bug). An old folk superstition says that if you let the lady beetle fly off unharmed, you will have good luck. If you have them living in your garden, consuming pests, you are indeed lucky! Other beneficials are equally intriguing, especially to children. Look for the praying mantis with its folded legs in a "prayer" position as it holds its prey; dragonflies, often with bright, metallic colors flashing in the sun as they swoop and dart; and green lacewings, with their filigree-like wings. Don't be fooled by the lacewings' delicate appearance. One voracious lacewing can consume up to 60 aphids per hour! There are many other beneficial insects such as big-eyed bugs and tiny wasps. If you decide to tolerate a few "bad bugs," such as aphids, on your plants, you will be providing a reason for beneficials to come to your garden. Indiscriminately spraying pesticides may kill beneficials as well as the target pest.

We advocate integrated pest management (IPM). IPM is simply a formalized way to practice all of the alternatives for controlling insects, including the environmentally friendly but effective use of beneficial insects, traps, cultivation practices, or even doing nothing at all.

Integrated Pest Management

An IPM program includes the following steps, which are described below:

1. Identify the pest.
2. Monitor the pest's population levels.
3. Decide how much damage is acceptable to you (for the plant's health and/or aesthetics).
4. Consider all options, including no control at all.
5. Keep accurate records.
6. Evaluate results and modify the program as needed.

1. Identify the Pest

Your best defense against excessive plant damage is to monitor your garden and learn who is a "good bug" and a "bad bug." Go out to the garden each morning and look at the plants. Examine the underside of leaves and fresh growth where pests are often found. If there is no damage, you can enjoy the view! What if you see holes in your cauliflower leaves? Encourage your children to play "detective" to find the culprit. Put the "suspect" insect in a jar with holes in the lid. Use a small stick or wear gloves to move the insect unless you are sure it won't bite or sting. Put an intact piece of the leaf or plant part that the insect was feeding on into the jar, taking care to avoid introducing other insects. Does more damage occur?

Examine the insect and the plant it was eating carefully. You may need a magnifying glass. Insect identification often starts by determining what type of damage was inflicted on the plant. For example, insects with sucking mouth parts, such as whiteflies, aphids and leafhoppers, cause the leaves to turn yellow and will leave sticky honeydew secretions. Ragged edges and holes in the leaves show that chewing insects, such as caterpillars, beetles, leafcutter bees or grasshoppers, have been feeding on your plants.

2. Monitor the Pest

Keep a close eye on the plant(s) for the next day or two. Does the insect population increase dramatically? Do the plants show increased damage? Have beneficials moved in?

3. Decide How Much Damage is Acceptable

Decide what, if anything, needs to be done. A few holes may not matter, especially if you plan to harvest soon. After all, you'll be eating the cauliflower head, not the outer leaves.

4. Control Options

Insects that chew leaves. The most significant garden pests with chewing mouth parts are tomato hornworms and cabbage loopers, which are large enough to be easily handpicked. Tomato hornworm larvae are bright green caterpillars about three inches long. They have white stripes on the body and a dark "horn" projecting from the rear. They are typically found on tomatoes, peppers and eggplant. Healthy plants can often sustain some feeding from tomato hornworms if their population isn't large.

Cabbage looper larvae are also green caterpillars but are smaller than hornworms. Cabbage loopers are about one to one-and-a-half-inches long with pale stripes running the length of their back. They "loop" as they crawl, forming a little arch with their bodies. They like to feed on members of the Cruciferae or cabbage family, including cabbage, broccoli, cauliflower, kale and others. Also watch for cutworms and armyworms.

Insects that suck nutrients out of leaves. Most insects with sucking mouth parts can be controlled with a strong spray from your hose, so try that first. Why indiscriminately spray insecticides? You may reduce the beneficial insect population, waste money and put unnecessary chemicals into the environment.

Aphids are tiny insects (1/16- to 1/8-inch long) that generally thrive in cooler weather. They may or may not have wings and are usually green or gray/black, depending upon the species and the plants they prefer to eat. Check annual flowers, beans, and the members of the cabbage family such as broccoli, bok choy, cabbage and kale. Aphids often cluster on new growth or buds and may cause yellowing, wilting or a sticky residue called honeydew.

Whiteflies are another tiny insect (less than 1/16-inch), but they are active in warmer weather, particularly late summer and early fall. The immature form of the whitefly looks like a scale and is attached to the underside of the plant's leaves, where it is sucking sap more voraciously than during its adult stage.

For particularly bad infestations of aphids or whiteflies, you might try a soapy water spray (see recipe below). Test a few leaves or one plant before spraying the whole crop. Be sure to spray the underside of the leaves, where many sucking insects, such as white-flies, reside. Spray in the early morning so that any soap solution won't burn the plants during the hotter parts of the day.

Another method of whitefly monitoring and control is to put "sticky" traps in the garden. You can purchase them from nurseries or make your own with yellow cardboard smeared on both sides with petroleum jelly. Whiteflies are attracted to the color yellow. They fly to it, get stuck and can't do any more damage to your plants.

Leafhoppers are about 1/8-inch long with strong jumping legs that allow them to move easily from plant to plant. Some leafhoppers spread a virus called "curly top" to tomatoes and some other vegetables. There is no cure for curly top once it strikes. "Floating row cover," a gauzy lightweight fabric that appears to "float" above the plants, can act as an insect barrier and provide a little shade. This control method has been used successfully to limit the aptly-named leafhoppers. They don't care for shade and should move on to find a brighter spot.

Soapy Water Spray Recipe

Use one teaspoon to two tablespoons of liquid detergent soap per gallon of water. Use regular detergent, not the extra concentrated types. Do not use dish soaps that contain lemon. The citric acid may burn plants. Start with the smaller amount of soap and increase if the insects aren't responding. Spray as often as needed. Keep records of when and how much was sprayed.

Slugs and snails. Little containers of any sugar, yeast and water mixture sunk below soil level will lure and drown slugs and snails. Barriers of diatomaceous earth or sawdust also keep them away.

Ants. If you have ants, citrus rind that has been finely ground into a slurry in a blender, or cream of wheat in its dry state, poured at the mouth of an ant hill should do the trick. Ground citrus only works during warm or hot weather; it must be used immediately after grinding to be effective. Note that many gardeners believe that ants help to improve the condition of the soil and don't mind sharing space with them, as long as they aren't the stinging kind. Contrary to common belief, with a few rare exceptions, the ants do not harm plants. They are more interested in feeding on the plant pests or the honeydew excreted by aphids and whiteflies.

Your very best defense against pest and disease is to grow strong, healthy plants. Vigorously growing plants will better tolerate attacks by insects and disease. Insects and diseases are attracted to stressed, unhealthy plants. Water appropriately to prevent disease and keep your soil as well conditioned as possible. Plant selection, soil improvement, proper watering and fertilizing

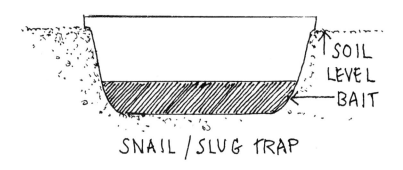

SOIL
LEVEL
BAIT

SNAIL / SLUG TRAP

have all been explained in earlier chapters. If you follow those guidelines, you should reduce the likelihood that your plants will be attacked by pests and disease. Other tips include:

❑ Look for cycles in pest populations and time your planting to avoid their peaks. For example, delay planting fall crops until the summer peak of the whitefly population has decreased. (Whiteflies don't reproduce as rapidly when the temperature starts to cool.)

❑ Apply water only to the crops, so weed seeds don't germinate in nearby areas.

❑ Get rid of overly abundant crops of weeds, which provide a food and shelter source for pests.

❑ Keep your garden free of sick or damaged plants, which invite pests. Remove plant debris and put it in your compost pile.

5. Keep Accurate Records

Keep a log of all insects you find. This is a fun activity for children. For example,

- When was the insect found?
- How many were there?
- What plant was the insect on?
- What kind of damage did the plant have?
- How quickly did the damage progress?
- What does the insect look like?
- How many legs does it have?
- What color is it?
- How big is it?
- Does it have wings?
- What, if any, control method was used?
- How much was applied and when?
- Did it work?

6. Evaluate Results and Modify Program as Needed

If you keep careful records, it will be relatively easy to determine what worked and what didn't. If for several days you tried a spray of water to get rid of aphids but their numbers increased, you may want to start with a low dose of soapy water. If that doesn't work, you might increase the amount of soap. Maybe you have counted an increase in the number of beneficials and will wait to see if they achieve the desired result. Keeping records makes this step fun and rewarding.

Crop Rotation

Crop rotation simply means planting different crops, or family of crops, in the same place season after season. Waiting two to three seasons or years before planting the same family is a good rule of thumb. An example of a family of crops would be the Cruciferae or cabbage family, including cabbage, broccoli, brussel sprouts, cauliflower, kale, radishes, turnips, rutabagas, bok choy and others.

Crop rotation is beneficial to the soil in two ways. First, alternating plants that feed heavily from the soil and thus deplete many of its nutrients (e.g., corn, tomatoes, squash, lettuce) with light feeders (e.g., turnips, carrots) or with legumes (e.g., peas, beans, alfalfa) that actually "fix" nitrogen in the soil, helps promote soil fertility. Secondly, by not planting the same crop, disease and insects that are plant- or family-specific don't have an opportunity to build up in the soil over time.

FLOATING ROW COVER

Preventing and Diagnosing Plant Problems

The most frequent cause of death for plants in an urban environment is well-meaning humans! We tend to select plants that are not well adapted to this environment. We don't take necessary steps at planting time, and either through over attention (too much water, fertilizer and pruning) or lack of attention, we allow the plant to become stressed and vulnerable to pests and disease. Often, correcting the management of the plants is sufficient to address the problem.

Many of the same cultural practices discussed in the previous chapter to prevent insect damage apply to preventing plant diseases. Soil improvement, proper watering practices, correct fertilizer application and choosing appropriate plant varieties for our climate all influence the health of your plants.

Preventing Problems

Think "Right Plant, Right Place" when purchasing plants. Select plants that are well adapted to this environment and are resistant to known pests. Place them in locations appropriate to their mature size so excessive pruning will not be necessary.

Prepare the soil appropriately (See Chapters 2 and 5). Dig a hole only as deep and twice as wide as the pot containing the plant. Plant at the same depth as it was in the pot. Do not plant too deep! (Tomatoes are the only exception to this rule. See Chapter 11 for information on planting tomatoes.)

Follow an appropriate schedule for plant care, irrigation and fertilization. Healthy plants resist pathogens that would damage or kill a stressed plant. Stressed plants actually attract insect pests.

Plant Disease Triangle

There are three essential elements to a plant problem: the Plant, the Environment and the Pathogen (a pathogen is an agent able to cause disease). These three elements make up the "Plant Disease Triangle." (See figure.)

Pay attention to the condition of your plants. Intervene early when you first start to see signs or symptoms of stress or disease. If you still have a problem, the following information can help you diagnose the cause.

Plant

Individual species have specific strengths, weaknesses and needs. They are adapted to thrive in a particular type of environment and may become stressed if their environmental needs are not met, e.g., compacted soil, inadequate or too much water, not enough or too much sunlight, temperature that is too warm or too cold. Specific types of plants are susceptible to certain live pathogens and not susceptible to others.

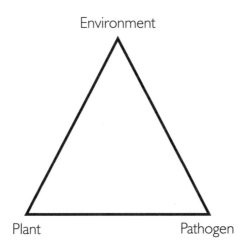

Plant Disease Triangle

Environment

The place where the plant grows has specific characteristics including the type of soil, irrigation, sunlight and weather. The plant may or may not be well adapted to these characteristics. The environment may be conducive to the action of certain pathogens and inhospitable to others.

Pathogen

Pathogens may be living organisms or nonliving factors. Some examples of living organisms include insects, animals, nematodes, plant parasites, fungi, bacteria and viruses. Generally, living pathogens are selective about the type of plant they feed upon, the damage they cause is progressive over time and they frequently leave evidence of their presence (fungal fruiting bodies, tunnels or galleries, droppings or dead insects). Some examples of nonliving pathogens include: mechanical or chemical injury, nutrient deficiency, weather (lightning, hail, sunburn) and pollution. In most cases nonliving pathogens cause a sudden onset of symptoms, the symptoms appear on a variety of plant types and the damage does not usually spread.

How to Diagnose Plant Problems

Diagnosis can be a complicated process requiring horticultural knowledge, experience, common sense, intuition, good judgement, and sometimes, good old-fashioned luck. Although it can be intimidating, there are specific strategies that you can use to successfully diagnose plant problems. Even if you are unable to diagnose the problem yourself, the following step-by-step system will improve your ability to provide the information needed by a professional to diagnose the problem.

1. Identify the Plant
  A. Know what is normal for the plant.
  B. Know the environmental and cultural needs of the plant.
  C. Know what pathogens the plant is susceptible to.

2. Define the Problems
A. Examine the physical evidence
1) Examine the entire plant (roots, stems and leaves). Based on knowledge of what is normal for this type of plant at this time of year, describe the abnormality.
2) Check the surrounding plants for similar symptoms.
3) Identify symptoms or signs of animals, insects or diseases.

B. Collect all the pertinent information
1) Description of plant's environment (sun, shade, soil, lawn, crushed granite).
2) Plant's age.
3) Any recent changes in cultural practices (planting, irrigating, fertilizing, pruning, applying pesticides).
4) What plants grew here previously? Is there a history of disease?
5) Onset of problem. When was it first noticed?
6) Weather (dust storms, lighting, rain, intense heat or cold, hail, strong winds).
7) Any unusual occurrences (the house next door burned down, irrigation line broke, chemical spill).

3. Look for Patterns
A. Pattern of symptoms on <u>individual</u> plant
1) Location of damage on plant
   a) New growth vs. old growth. Is the plant growing out of the damage? Some nutrients are translocated within the plant so the plant can "rob" the older leaves to feed the new; thus, the symptoms appear on the old growth. Other nutrients do not move within the plant so deficiency symptoms show up on the new growth.
   b) Which side of plant (west vs. east; interior vs. exterior)? Damage only on the west side may indicate sunburn; damage only on the external leaves may indicate chemical drift.
2) Progression within plant and/or to other plants
   a) Progressive spread of damage on a plant, onto other plants or over an area with time generally indicates the damage was caused by a living organism.

b) If the damage occurs and does not spread to other plants or other parts of the affected plant, and if there is a clear line of demarcation between damaged and undamaged tissues, it is likely that the plant was damaged by nonliving factors (weather, chemical, mechanical damage).

B. Pattern of <u>multiple</u> plants affected within an environment
1) Types of plants affected
   a) Non-uniform damage to only one particular type of plant indicates a living pathogen (insect or disease).
   b) Uniform damage to a large area and several different types of plants indicates a nonliving pathogen (weather, mechanical or chemical factors).
2) Any relationship between the location of damaged plants and the watering pattern?

4. Make a tentative diagnosis
A. Start with a good reference book for your climate. Most are indexed by plant. Some are also indexed by causal agent.
B. Look up the plant in the index.
C. Review the pathogens listed.
D. Select and read about likely options.
E. Compare the information that you have gathered to the description in the book.
F. Identify the causal agent. If you are unable to diagnose the problem, take a sample to your local nursery or Cooperative Extension office to get a professional opinion.

5. Develop a plan for managing the problem
A. Based on the identification of the plant, determine general plant care strategies. A healthy, unstressed plant is less vulnerable to disease.
B. Use the disease triangle to identify the most effective method of managing the problem. It may be possible to modify the environment to have it better meet the needs of the plant or to make it inhospitable to the pathogen. It may be possible to remove or directly manage the pathogen. It may be necessary to replace the plant with one better adapted to the environment and less vulnerable to the pathogen.

Vegetables, Flowers & Herbs

The gardening practices described throughout this book can help you to grow just about any type of plant, but this chapter provides additional material specific to vegetables, flowers or herbs. Other sources of information include local gardening clubs, County Cooperative Extension offices, Web sites, e-mail list serves and friendly gardeners. We've never met a gardener who didn't enjoy sharing details of a gardening venture!

Vegetables

Nothing tastes better than vegetables picked fresh from your own garden. Here in the low desert you can harvest fresh vegetables almost year round. However, we have two distinct growing seasons. Cool-season vegetables are those from which we eat the roots, stems and leaves (e.g., carrots and spinach). They thrive from September to April with short days and cool nights. Warm-season vegetables are those from which we eat the fruit (e.g., melons and tomatoes). They grow from March to October, with some summer hiatus. The major exception to this rule-of-thumb is peas, which are planted and harvested during the cool season.

Cool-season vegetables (beets, broccoli, cabbage, carrots, lettuce and other greens, onions, garlic, peas, radishes and turnips) all do best planted in the fall and allowed to mature through the winter and spring. Warm temperatures and longer day length often trigger flowering and the end of their productivity.

Warm-season vegetables (beans, cucumbers, eggplant, melons, peppers, pumpkin, squash, sweet corn, sweet potatoes and tomatoes) require warm temperatures and longer days to flower and set fruit. These vegetables take longer to grow since they are a product of the complete plant life cycle (seed to plant to flower to fruit to seed). It's important to select varieties that mature quickly so they can flower and set fruit before the highest temperatures hit. Tomato and pepper pollens are not viable at high temperatures, so once it hits 90 degrees, not much fruit will be set on the plant. The fruit that has already been pollinated will continue to grow and ripen, but new flowers will not be pollinated and set.

Many crops do well when planted directly into the garden from seed (beans, carrots, peas, squash, sunflowers and most root crops). However, some plants that take longer to grow may do better if started from seed in containers in a greenhouse or indoors in bright light. They will then be ready for transplanting into the garden as soon as the temperature is right, thus getting a jumpstart on the season. Vegetables that do well as transplants include broccoli, cabbage, cauliflower, eggplant, peppers, sweet potatoes and tomatoes. Consult the Vegetable Planting Calendar, which lists crops that are better planted as seeds or transplants and also contains a range of "best dates" for planting. These timeframes provide for the greatest probability of success, but realize that yearly weather conditions and microclimates (specific site conditions such as amount of sunlight and temperature) can vary considerably. Adjust these dates for your specific growing conditions.

Soil and Fertilizer

Vegetables thrive in rich, well-draining soil that has been amended with plenty of organic matter. Follow the guidelines in Chapters 2 and 5 for improving and preparing the soil and you'll be ready to plant a vegetable garden. Incorporate a three- to six-inch layer of organic matter into your soil to a depth of eight to twelve inches before *each* planting season in the spring and fall.

Fertilizer—what kind and how much to add—is one of those interesting topics in which a dozen gardeners can express a dozen opinions. Experienced gardeners who have been amending their soil with large amounts of organic matter for at least several years often find that they no longer need to add fertilizer to their vegetable beds. Others prefer to incorporate fertilizer into the soil before each planting. Still others like to add fertilizer as a "side dressing" to plants after they've become established to provide a boost during their growing peak.

Many vegetables, including corn, lettuce, spinach, chard, kale and other greens, are heavy nitrogen feeders and if the soil is poor or this is the first garden you've planted in that area, your vegetables may benefit from a side dressing of a nitrogen fertilizer halfway through the growing season. Chapter 2 contains specific details on different types of fertilizer. Dig the fertilizer into the soil a few inches from the plant. Be careful to keep it away from the roots to prevent burning. If possible, incorporate the fertilizer into moist soil, which also helps prevent burning.

Fruiting crops, such as tomatoes and peppers, require phosphorous to flower and set fruit. Because phosphorous doesn't move readily through the soil as does nitrogen, it should be mixed into the soil before planting or placed at the bottom of planting holes so the plant's roots have ready access to it.

Because there are so many variables involved—the condition of the soil, plant species, fertilizer type (dry, slow release, liquid), weather, your garden's microclimate—it's difficult to recommend a specific fertilizer program. Be sure to follow label directions on the fertilizer's container. Using too much fertilizer can do more damage than using too little. Let your plants and your "eye" determine what is needed. Do leafy vegetables look green and healthy? Are flowers forming on fruiting plants? Diagnosing Plant Problems in Appendix B can help determine nutrient deficiencies.

Insects

If you monitor the plants on a regular basis, you can generally take care of any "invasions" before they do much damage. Review Chapter 9, which contains information on pests often found in vegetable gardens, as well as easy ways to manage them without the use of pesticides.

There are also things you can do to prevent problems from even starting, such as choosing varieties that are bred to be disease and pest resistant. Initials following the plant variety name indicate resistance to a specific problem. This information is found on the seed packet or in catalog descriptions.

Another strategy is to plant at a time that will help to avoid known pest populations. For example, whiteflies generally increase in number around August and September and decline as temperatures cool. Some gardeners delay fall planting until October to give the plants a break from the sap-sucking whiteflies. However, existing melon and squash plants are quick to be attacked when whiteflies appear.

Varieties

Seed companies offer so many new varieties each year that it's hard to maintain a current list of vegetables that will do well in our conditions. In addition to pest and disease resistance, here's what to look for when choosing varieties for a desert garden.

With our relatively short growing seasons, it's important to plant varieties that mature quickly so they can complete their life cycle. Check out seed catalog descriptions for "days to maturity" and those with "early" in their name, which denotes crops that are ready for harvesting early in the season.

Smaller fruits, (e.g., cherry tomatoes), will generally do much better than the larger ones (e.g., beefsteak tomatoes), which take longer to mature and often crack and blister in the intense sun. Choose smaller varieties that are adapted to heat. Tomatoes that don't need to be staked do well in the desert, as their foliage provides shade for the rest of the plant, lowering the temperature and raising the humidity.

Carrots with blunt ends do better in dense, clay soil than those that are long and tapered. Leaf lettuce performs better than head lettuce. Many local gardeners think that vining varieties of beans and peas taste better than bush varieties. Small beets have a more pleasing texture than large beets, which can get "woody."

Tips

❑ Before transplanting tomatoes, remove all the leaves below the top two nodes. (Nodes are "joints" where new leaves arise. Dig a shallow trench, put a phosphorous source in the bottom and place the plant on its side in the hole. Bury it up to the last two nodes. As tomatoes are able to sprout roots along the entire buried stem, this method gives the plant an added advantage.

❑ Some crops that continue to grow and can be harvested during the hot summer include Armenian cucumbers, blackeyed peas, corn, eggplant (best with afternoon shade to protect fruit from burning), melons, okra, squash, Swiss chard and sunflowers. If tomatoes are protected with shade, they may continue fruiting in the fall.

❑ Vining crops, such as cucumbers, canteloupes, and small watermelons can hang on sturdy trellises to save space and provide shade.

❑ Floating row cover will help protect seeds and plants from insects and birds. It also creates a warmer environment, similar to a mini-greenhouse, to provide a jumpstart if you can't wait to start planting at the end of winter/early spring. During the hot months, it provides a little shade protection and helps keep soil from drying out so quickly.

❑ Many gardeners like to maximize production of tomatoes before hot weather sets in. They use Wall O' Waters®, a product that's name describes it well. A self-standing plastic cylinder has compartments that the gardener fills with water. The young plant grows in the ground, surrounded by the cyclinder. The water heats up during the day from the sun's warmth and acts as an insulator or mini-greenhouse.

❑ Corn relies on wind pollination, so you need enough plants in a block grouping to ensure pollination. The minimum size for a plot is 16 to 36 square feet, depending on a particular variety's stalk size. The square-foot method described earlier works well with corn in the desert as it reduces evaporation. If planted in traditional rows, corn on the south or west sides drys out sooner, suffers windburn or sunburn, becomes stunted and is less likely to be pollinated. Plant only one variety because cross-fertilization of different varieties can impact the taste and texture of this season's crop.

Flowers

Almost all vegetables are classified as annuals (asparagus and artichoke being notable exceptions), but flowers can be annuals, perennials or biennials.

Annuals

Annual flowers complete their life cycle—vegetative plant, bloom, setting seed, to death of the plant—in one growing season.

Most annuals need to be replanted each year, but others easily resow themselves. Their seed is scattered by wind, weather and wildlife, to pop up the next season when conditions are favorable. These unexpected visitors are called "volunteers" and can be a delight or a source of frustration, depending on your outlook and how rigidly you follow the garden's original design! Larkspur, cornflower, poppies, desert marigold, calendula, scarlet flax, gaillardia and Johnny-jump-ups are a few flowers that are easy to grow and readily reseed.

Gardeners love annuals for their riotous colors. They perform quickly, especially if transplants are used, and provide relatively long periods of bloom. Annuals are particularly useful to conceal bare spots while landscape plants become established; create masses of color as a focal point; or fill containers to establish a cheerful presence at entryways and entertainment areas, including patios and pool decks.

At the end of the annual's growing season, the entire plant is put in the compost pile and something else can take its place. Many gardeners find it fun to experiment with annuals. If you don't like the color combinations you chose, plant something else next season. The Flower Planting Guide in this book lists annual and perennial flowers, the best time to plant, when they flower, flower color and much more.

Perennials

Once established, perennial flowers bloom each season for several years or more, depending on the species and growing conditions. Some die back to the ground in their off-season; others retain foliage year around. In the low desert, perennial off-seasons are usually during the intense heat of summer and the colder winter months.

You may notice that the Flower Planting Guide categorizes many of your favorite perennials from "back home" as annuals. That's because they don't receive enough winter cold for dormancy or can't survive our summer heat (without inordinate amounts of care) and are more successfully grown in the low desert as annuals.

Perennials require more maintenance than do annuals. They may need to be cut back during their off-season, and divided and replanted as they increase in size. Some of their blooms are tall or heavy enough to require staking. Typically, perennial flower beds are designed to have different combinations of flowers blooming as the year progresses. Unlike annuals, which have a lengthy flowering period, most perennials display peak blossoms for a two- or three-week period. Thus, the design of a perennial garden should take into account when the flowers bloom, as well as their color, height and leaf texture.

Biennials

Biennials grow vegetatively in their first year, flower in the second year and typically die after flowering. Because we have two growing seasons here, biennials may complete their entire life cycle in one year. Hollyhocks may grow as biennials in the low desert, but most flowers will act as annuals or perennials.

Soil and Fertilizer

Most flowers prefer a nutrient-rich, well-drained soil (nobody likes wet feet). Follow the information in Chapters 2 and 5 and you can create dark, crumbly soil in which your flowers will thrive. If this is your first attempt or if your patch of "hardrock" fills you with despair, you might want to concentrate on the flowers marked as "Wildflowers" or "Reseeds" in the Planting Guide. Many of these don't require as rich a soil, preferring a more "native" environment.

Other annual flowers, like vegetables, are heavy "eaters" and will require nitrogen for vegetative growth and phosphorous for healthy roots and flowers. (See the sections on Macronutrients and Fertilizers in Chapter 2 for more details.) However, too much nitrogen may create a healthy green, vigorous plant, with few flowers. Phosphorous is not water soluble and thus can not move easily through the soil. It needs to be placed deeply enough in the soil so the plant's roots can easily take it up. Thus, it should be mixed into the soil in the root zone before planting, or dug into side trenches if required after the plant is established. If plants are in the ground, fertilizer is best applied to moist soil to help prevent "burning" delicate roots. Perennial flowers should be fertilized when you see the first flush of new growth. Don't fertilize when the plant is going into dormancy.

Because there are so many variables involved—the condition of the soil, plant species, fertilizer type (dry, slow release, liquid), weather, your garden's microclimate—there is no magic formula for applying fertilizer. Follow the directions on the label of the fertilizer you choose. Depending on your conditions, you may need to add fertilizer as often as every six weeks or so during the flowers' peak growing season. If you have nutrient-rich soil that is well prepared before planting, additional fertilizer may not be required. Consider keeping a garden journal, noting what kind of fertilizer you used, how much and when it was applied. Keep an eye on your plants. Do they look green and healthy? Do buds and flowers form? Let your plants and your "eye" determine what is needed. Diagnosing Plant Problems in Appendix B provides a handy guide to unhealthy symptoms and possible causes.

Flowers grown in containers need a regular schedule of fertilizer or a timed-release fertilizer mixed in at planting time. Some Master Gardeners recommend applying a diluted fertilizer with each watering in cooler weather. In hot weather, you may need to water daily, so cut back on fertilizer to once a week. This is only a guide. The size of the plants and container will determine fertilizer needs.

Tips

❑ Remember that the low desert provides avid gardeners with two distinct growing seasons: a warm season in which flowers can be planted from approximately March through May, some of which will bloom through the summer; and a cool season in which plants grow and bloom from approximately September through April, or until temperatures heat up.

❑ Perennial flowers show to their best advantage when planted in groups of odd numbers (three, five, seven) in a drifting effect. Annuals look great when massed together for maximum color effect, although they can also work grouped in odd numbers. Single plants of many varieties tend to look disorganized. Avoid straight rows for a more natural appearance. Take a look at how plants grow in nature—when's the last time you saw a straight line? However, smaller, low-growing plants can work well as a continuous border along the front of a bed with taller flowers behind in two or three "layers."

❑ "Deadheading" is the term used for removing spent blossoms. Cutting or pinching off the dead flowers on a weekly basis prolongs the blooming period. Toss the dead flowers into your compost pile.

❑ White flowers show well at dusk. Use them near patios, entryways and entertainment areas where they can be shown to best advantage.

❑ Some annuals reseed themselves quite readily. You may either enjoy future generations of these flower volunteers in your garden, or if not wanted, remove the spent blossoms before seeds mature and drop. Reseeded annuals can be great for gifts or to sell at yard sales.

❑ When planting a one-sided bed (next to a wall, for example), put taller plants in back. If the flower bed can be seen from two sides, tall growers look best in the center so they don't conceal smaller plants.

❑ Use "dwarf" varieties for smaller spaces or containers.

Herbs

Many people assume that herbs need shade, but like most vegetables and flowers, they should receive at least 6-8 hours of sunlight each day for optimum performance. Some afternoon shade can help prolong production during our intense summer heat.

Soil and Fertilizer

Most herbs will thrive in soil that has been well amended with organic matter as described in the section on soil structure. Good drainage is important for most herbs, but it's a must for herbs that originated in the Mediterranean and similar regions where the soil is typically dry and rocky. Examples of these herbs include such favorites as oregano, sage, lavender, rosemary, thyme, santolina, artemisia, tarragon and fennel.

Herbs don't require a specific fertilizing program. Similar to overwatering, overfertilizing promotes lush green growth, but diminishes flavor and scent because the herbs' oils aren't as concentrated. If you continue to improve your soil quality by adding organic matter twice a year, you should not need additional fertilizer for your herb plants.

When to plant

Just as we discussed with vegetables and flowers, there are also two distinct growing seasons for herbs, with some performing better in warmer temperatures and others preferring the cooler months. If you are a beginning gardener, you might want to try planting winter hardy herbs in the fall to allow their roots plenty of time to develop before the summer heat arrives.

Herbs, like flowers, can be annuals, perennials or biennials. Annuals complete their life cycle in one growing season; perennials live several years or more; and biennials grow the first year, bloom in the second year and die after flowering. Basil is a favorite culinary herb that needs to be resown each year; lavender's beautiful flowers are perennial. Check the Herb Planting Calendar in Appendix C, which lists herbs by type and also provides the best time of year to plant.

Watering and Tending

Most herbs don't require as much water as do vegetables and flowers. Many newcomers to desert gardening tend to overwater plants, perhaps as a reaction to living in such a dry climate. In fact, many more herb plants are killed due to overwatering than from other factors. Herbs will reward you with better flavor and scent—and live longer—if not overwatered.

Herbs can become leggy if not pinched or trimmed back regularly. Harvesting will promote a compact growth habit with fresh, tender leaves. Don't cut more than one-third of the plant at any time. If you can't use all of the fresh herbs, dry or freeze them for later use, or tie up a *bouquet garni* for friends. A bouquet garni is simply a few fresh herb sprigs tied with string or tucked into a piece of cheesecloth. Used to flavor soups and stews, the bouquet garni can be easily removed before serving, leaving behind its flavor but not bits of plant material. People who have never used fresh herbs will be amazed at how they enhance a favorite recipe.

As colder weather approaches, reduce watering and harvesting of perennial herbs. This allows plants a chance to "harden off" to reduce potential frost damage. When weather begins warming with the return of spring, old woody growth and any frost damage can be pruned when fresh green sprouts begin to show.

Insects

If the herb plants are healthy, insects generally do minimal damage. One of the lovely benefits of herbs is that their flowers attract many beneficial insects. Insects that either act as pollinators or destroy other insects that are eating your plants are terrific visitors to welcome to your garden. For example, bees are industrious pollinators that are attracted to most herbs in flower. Many gardeners intersperse herb plants among their vegetables to encourage bees to transfer pollen from male to female flowers for such fruiting vegetables as tomatoes, squash and cucumbers.

If possible, plant a wide variety of herbs to provide food and shelter for beneficial insects. Basil, chamomile, thyme, lavender and mint as well as flowering plants from the carrot (*Umbelliferae*) family such as dill, chervil, fennel and parsley are excellent plants to attract beneficials.

Tips

❑ Herbs that originated in the Mediterranean region's dry, alkaline soils are usually easy growers for beginners because they thrive in full sun and tolerate our arid conditions without much fuss. Mediterranean herbs used in cooking include oregano, sage, rosemary, thyme and fennel. Lavender and artemisia are terrific for scent and floral bouquets. Santolina's low, dense growing habit works especially well in knot gardens. Other easy herbs for beginners include basil, lemon grass and garlic chives, but they may require more water than the others listed.

❑ Some herbs are amazingly aggressive, sending out roots in all directions, which can overwhelm any neighboring plants. Herbs with invasive root structures include mints and some oreganos, such as Greek, Italian, and Dwarf Creeping. However, mints are by far the more invasive. Control these herbs by planting them in large plastic pots that have the bottom cut out. Sink the pot in the garden leaving about two inches of the container's rim above ground level. Use at least a three-gallon, and preferably a five-gallon pot to allow enough room for an attractive plant to grow. Fill the pot with compost-enriched soil for best results.

❑ Other herbs are prolific seed producers, scattering their progeny far afield. You might want to remove seed heads before they ripen and start falling, drifting and scattering everywhere. Dill, garlic chives, mint, fennel, catnip, chamomile, chicory, epazote and horehound are known to pop up in great quantity the following year. Harvest their seeds to share with fellow gardeners.

How to Save Seeds

Save seeds from your nonhybrid plants so that you won't have to purchase them next year. Allow a few plants to "go to seed." For flowers and vegetables that reproduce with flowerheads (lettuce and other greens), tie small paper bags over the plant's flowerheads. The bag will catch the seeds as they fall. (Punch a few tiny holes in the bag to provide air circulation.) For fruiting vegetables that produce seeds within (tomatoes), allow the fruit to become very ripe, but not rotten, on the vine before harvesting it for seeds.

Collect seeds on a dry, sunny day after any morning dew is gone. Moisture will encourage seeds to rot. Dry seeds for a week on sheets of newspaper. Clean the seeds of excess leaves, stems or insects. Store in an airtight container in the refrigerator or in a cool, dry place.

Don't save seeds from hybrids; they will not develop true to the parent plant.

Appendices

A. References

B. Diagnosing Plant Problems

C. Planting Calendars
   Vegetables
   Herbs
   Flowers

References

Backyard Composting. Your Complete Guide to Recycling Yard Clippings. Harmonious Technologies, 1992. Harmonius Press, Ojai, CA.

Better Homes and Gardens Gardening Naturally: A Guide to Growing Chemical Free Flowers, Vegetables, and Herbs. Ann Reilly, 1993. Michael Friedman Publishing Group, New York.

The Complete Book of Herbs: A practical guide to growing & using herbs. Lesley Bremness, 1988. Viking Penguin, New York.

Desert Gardening: Fruits and Vegetables: The Complete Guide. George Brookbank, 1991. Fisher Books, Tucson, AZ.

Desert Harvest: A Guide to Vegetable Production in Arid Lands. Jane Nyhuis, 1982. Growing Connections, Tucson, AZ, 520-298-9101.

Desert Wildflowers. Desert Botanical Garden staff, 1988. Arizona Highways/Arizona Department of Transportation, Phoenix.

Diseases of Trees and Shrubs. W.A. Sinclair, H.H. Lyon, and W.T. Johnson, 1987. Cornell University Press, Ithaca, NY.

Don't Waste Your Wastes—Compost 'em. Bert Whitehead, 1991. Sunnyvale Press, Mesquite, TX.

Drip Irrigation for Every Landscape and All Climates. Robert Kourik, 1992. Metamorphic Press, Santa Rosa, CA.

Herbs Grow in the Desert Southwest. Charlie Humme, 1994. Fresh Touch Gardens Press, Peoria, AZ.

Insects that Feed on Trees and Shrubs. W.T. Johnson and H.H. Lyon, 1991. Cornell University Press, Ithaca, NY.

Introduction to Permaculture. Bill Mollison with Reny Mia Slay, 1994. Tagari Publications, Tyalgum, Australia. Distributed by Permaculture Resources, P.O. Box 65, Califon, NJ 07830, 800-832-6285.

Landscaping for Desert Wildlife. Carolyn Engel-Wilson, 1992. Arizona Game and Fish Department, Phoenix, AZ, 602-789-3236.

Learning About & Living With Insects of the Southwest. Floyd Werner and Carl Olson, 1995. Fisher Press, Tucson, AZ.

Let It Rot! The Gardener's Guide to Composting. Stu Campbell, 1990. Storey Communications, Pownal, VT.

The Low Desert Herb Gardening Handbook. Anne Fischer, 1997. Arizona Herb Association, P.O. Box 63101, Phoenix, AZ, 85082-3101.

The Low-Water Flower Gardener. Eric A. Johnson and Scott Millard, 1993. Millard Publishing Services, Tucson, AZ.

Master Gardener Entomology Manual. Dave Langston and Roberta Gibson, 1995. College of Agriculture, University of Arizona, Tucson, AZ.

Master Gardener Horticultural Communicator. Newsletter published six times a year by Maricopa County Cooperative Extension, 4341 E. Broadway Road, Phoenix, AZ 85040, 602-470-8086, http://ag.arizona.edu/maricopa/garden/.

Nutrient Deficiencies and Toxicities in Crop Plants. W.F. Bennett, 1993. American Phytopathological Society Press, St. Paul, MN.

The Plant Disease Clinic & Field Diagnosis of Abiotic Diseases. M.C. Shurtleff & C.W. Averre, 1996. American Phytopathological Society Press, St. Paul, MN.

Rodale's Chemical-Free Yard & Garden: The Ultimate Authority. Anna Carr, et al., 1991. Rodale Press, Emmaus, PA.

Rodale's Illustrated Encyclopedia of Herbs. Claire Kowalchik and William H. Hylton, Editors, 1987. Rodale Press, Emmaus, PA.

Square Foot Gardening. Mel Bartholomew, 1981. Rodale Press, Emmaus, PA. Also available in a three-volume video set (50 minutes each).

Sunset Annuals. Sunset Editors, 1992. Sunset Publishing Corporation, Menlo Park, CA.

Sunset Perennials. Sunset Editors, 1992. Sunset Publishing Corporation, Menlo Park, CA.

Sunset Western Garden Book. Sunset Editors, 1995. Sunset Publishing Corporation, Menlo Park, CA.

Warm-Climate Gardening: Tips, Techniques, Plans, Projects for Humid or Dry Conditions. Barbara Pleasant, 1993. Storey Communications, Pownal, VT.

World Wide Web/Internet

http://ag.arizona.edu/maricopa/garden/
The Maricopa County Home Horticulture Website provides a wide variety of information specific to gardening in the low desert.

http://ag.arizona.edu/maricopa/garden/html/general/lists.htm
Post questions, gather ideas or read information from gardeners around the Southwest on a variety of list serves.

http://ag.arizona.edu/maricopa/garden/html/general/compost.htm
Where to find free or inexpensive compost bins.

http://ag.arizona.edu/PLP/plpext/index.html
The University of Arizona Cooperative Extension Plant Pathology Website.

http://ag.arizona.edu/gardening
Arid Southwest gardening information and links to other sites from the College of Agriculture and Life Sciences, University of Arizona.

Diagnosing Plant Problems

This information was adapted from the "Arizona Master Gardener Diagnostic Key," written by Dr. Deborah J. Young, Associate Director, Programs, The University of Arizona Cooperative Extension. Check with your Extension office for information on local plant problems.

Symptoms	Possible Causes	Controls
Seedlings don't emerge	❑ Dry soil ❑ Seeds washed away ❑ Birds ate them ❑ Incorrect planting depth ❑ Slow germination due to weather ❑ Damping off (fungal disease)	✓ Supply water ✓ Don't overwater ✓ Cover seed bed ✓ Plant 2–3 times deeper than seed size ✓ Check planting calendars ✓ Don't overwater; use seeds treated with fungicide; start seeds in sterile potting mix and clean pots
Seedlings wilt; fall over	❑ Dry soil ❑ Damping off (fungal disease)	✓ Supply water ✓ Same as above
Seedlings chewed; leaves shredded or stripped	❑ Slugs ❑ Various insects ❑ Rodents, rabbits, birds	✓ Use IPM methods ✓ Use IPM methods ✓ Fence garden; cover seedlings
Newer leaves yellow; veins remain green	❑ Iron deficiency or plant roots unable to absorb iron	✓ Add iron sulfate or iron chelate to soil

Symptoms	Possible Causes	Controls
General leaf yellowing	❏ Nitrogen deficiency ❏ Insufficient light	✓ Add nitrogen fertilizer; add organic matter ✓ Thin plants; transplant to better location
Wilted plants; bottom leaves may yellow	❏ Dry soil ❏ Root rot ❏ Vascular wilt (fungal disease) ❏ Root knot nematode ❏ Water-logged soil	✓ Supply water ✓ Don't overwater; remove old plant debris; rotate crops ✓ Plant resistant varieties; rotate crops ✓ Rotate crops; add high level of organic matter; soil solarization ✓ Improve drainage
Plants grow slowly; leaves light green	❏ Insufficient light ❏ Cool weather ❏ Improper pH ❏ Excess water ❏ Insufficient nitrogen	✓ Thin plants; don't plant in shade ✓ Check planting calendar ✓ Amend soil ✓ Don't overwater; improve drainage ✓ Add nitrogen fertilizer
Leaves with yellow-green mottle pattern; may be puckered and plants stunted	❏ Virus disease	✓ Plant resistant varieties; weed control; remove affected plants and debris; there is no cure
Leaves stippled with tiny white spots	❏ Spider mites ❏ Air pollution (ozone)	✓ Use IPM techniques
White powdery growth on leaf surfaces	❏ Powdery mildew (fungal disease)	✓ Improve air circulation; increase sunlight until temperatures exceed 90 degrees; use sulfur dust

Symptoms	Possible Causes	Controls
Leaf margins turn brown and shrivel	❏ Dry soil ❏ Fertilizer or salt burn ❏ Potassium deficiency ❏ Cold injury	✓ Supply water ✓ Soil test for soluble salts; don't overapply fertilizer; apply gypsum and flush soil with water ✓ Amend soil as needed ✓ Protect from frost
Discrete brown spots; some may grow and merge with others	❏ Fungal or bacterial leaf spot disease ❏ Chemical injury	✓ Submit sample for diagnosis ✓ Contact custodian about pesticide/herbicide use that may have "drifted"
Leaves curled, puckered or distorted	❏ Herbicide injury ❏ Virus disease ❏ Aphids	✓ Contact custodian about lawn herbicides that may have drifted; apply on calm days only ✓ Plant resistant varieties; weed control; remove affected plants and debris ✓ Use IPM techniques
Transplants wilt	❏ Shock due to root damage or drying ❏ Shock due to temperature extremes	✓ Trim top growth on larger plants to compensate for root loss ✓ Provide shade ✓ Plant in late afternoon
Poor fruit yield; small fruit; poor taste	❏ Uneven moisture ❏ Poor soil fertility	✓ Supply water during dry periods ✓ Amend soil as needed
Large, sunken watersoaked spot on blossom end of fruit; spot turns black; mold may grow	❏ Blossom end rot, due to calcium deficiency	✓ Developing fruits receive uneven moisture; supply water during dry periods; mulch ✓ Apply gypsum

Planting Calendars

Planting dates are suggested guidelines that should provide the highest probability of success; however, weather conditions vary by year and location, and planting dates should be adjusted accordingly. This material was adapted from the "Maricopa County Cooperative Extension Fruit and Vegetable Garden Planting Guide for the Low Desert," prepared by Lucy K. Bradley, Urban Horticulture Agent, and Kai Umeda, Vegetable Crops Agent. It indicates a range of planting dates for seeds (S) and transplants (T). Fruits & Vegetables for July–December follow, as do Planting Calendars for Herbs and Flowers.

Planting Calendar—Fruits & Vegetables January–June

Fruit or Vegetable	Days to Harvest	Jan 1	Jan 15	Feb 1	Feb 15	Mar 1	Mar 15	Apr 1	Apr 15	May 1	May 15	Jun 1	Jun 15
Artichoke, Globe	1 year		T	T	T	T	T						
Artichoke, Jerusalem	6–8 months		T	T	T	T	T	T	T	T	T		
Asparagus	1–2 years	T	T	T									
Beans, Lima	60–100							S	S				
Beans, Pinto	60–90												
Beans, Snap	60–90							S	S	S			
Beets	60–80	S	S	S	S	S							
Blackeyed Peas	90–120							S	S	S			
Bok Choy	45	S	S	S	S								

S Seeds **T** Transplants

Planting Calendar—Fruits & Vegetables
January–June

Fruit or Vegetable	Days to Harvest	Jan 1	Jan 15	Feb 1	Feb 15	Mar 1	Mar 15	Apr 1	Apr 15	May 1	May 15	Jun 1	Jun 15
Broccoli	T: 90–100 S: 120–130	T S	T										
Brussel Sprouts	T: 100–120 S: 130–150												
Cabbage	T: 80–90 S: 120–130	T S	T										
Cabbage, Chinese	T: 45 S: 70–80	T S	T										
Carrots	60–100	S	S	S	S	S	S	S	S				
Cauliflower	T: 90–100 S: 120–130	T S	T										
Celery	120–150												
Chard	60–90	T S	T S	T									
Collards	80	S	S	S	S								
Corn, Sweet	70–90					S	S	S					
Cucumbers	60–90					S	S	S	S	S			
Cucumbers, Armenian	55											S	S
Eggplant	70–120					T	T						
Endive	80–120												
Jicama	180–210					S	S	S	S				
Kale	60–90												
Kohlrabi	T: 45–60 S: 50–60	T	T	T									
Lettuce, Head	50–100	T S	T S	T									
Lettuce, Leaf	50–90	T S	T S	T S	T								
Leek	180–200	S	S										

S Seeds **T** Transplants

Planting Calendar—Fruits & Vegetables
January–June

Fruit or Vegetable	Days to Harvest	Jan 1	Jan 15	Feb 1	Feb 15	Mar 1	Mar 15	Apr 1	Apr 15	May 1	May 15	Jun 1	Jun 15
Melon, Musk Cantaloupe	80–120				S	S	S	S	S	S	S	S	S
Melon, Watermelon	90–120				S	S	S						
Mustard Greens	35–45	S	S	S	S								
Okra	70–100						S	S	S	S	S		
Onions, Bulb	S: 7–8 mon. Sets: 4-5 mon.			Sets									
Onions, Green	90–100	S	S	S	S	S	S	S	S				
Parsnips	100–120												
Peanuts	5 months						S	S	S				
Peas	Sep: 60–120 Nov: 120–150	S	S	S	S								
Peppers	90–120				T	T	T						
Potatoes	90–120	S	S	S	S								
Potatoes, Sweet	120–160									T	T	T	T
Pumpkin	90–120					S	S						
Radishes	40–60	S	S	S	S	S	S	S	S				
Rutabagas	100–120		S										
Spinach	40–90	S	S	S	S								
Squash, Summer	60–90					S	S	S	S				
Squash, Winter	90–120					S	S						
Tomatoes	50–120				T	T	T						
Turnips	90–120	S	S	S	S								

S Seeds **T** Transplants

Planting Calendar—Fruits & Vegetables
July–December

Fruit or Vegetable	Days to Harvest	Jul 1	Jul 15	Aug 1	Aug 15	Sep 1	Sep 15	Oct 1	Oct 15	Nov 1	Nov 15	Dec 1	Dec 15
Artichoke, Globe	1 year												
Artichoke, Jerusalem	6–8 months												
Asparagus	1–2 years									T	T	T	T
Beans, Lima	60–100												
Beans, Pinto	60–90			S									
Beans, Snap	60–90				S	S							
Beets	60–80					S	S	S	S	S	S	S	S
Blackeyed Peas	90–120												
Bok Choy	45					S	S	S	S	S	S	S	S
Broccoli	T: 90–100 S: 120–130					S	S	T S	T S	T S	T S	T S	T S
Brussel Sprouts	T: 100–120 S: 130–150					S	T S	T S	T S	T S	T	T	
Cabbage	T: 80–90 S: 120–130					S	S	T S	T S	T S	T S	T S	T S
Cabbage, Chinese	T: 45 S: 70–80					S	S	T S	T S	T S	T S	T S	T S
Carrots	60–100				S	S	S	S	S	S	S	S	S
Cauliflower	T: 90–100 S: 120–130					S	T S	T S	T S	T S	T S	T S	T S
Celery	120–150					S	T S	T S	T S				
Chard	60–90						T S	T S	T S	T S	T S		
Collards	80					S	S	S	S	S	S	S	S
Corn, Sweet	70–90			S	S	S							
Cucumbers	60–90					S	S	S					

S Seeds **T** Transplants

Planting Calendar—Fruits & Vegetables
July–December

Fruit or Vegetable	Days to Harvest	Jul 1	Jul 15	Aug 1	Aug 15	Sep 1	Sep 15	Oct 1	Oct 15	Nov 1	Nov 15	Dec 1	Dec 15
Cucumbers, Armenian	55	S											
Eggplant	70–120												
Endive	80–120					S	S	S	S	S			
Jicama	180–210												
Kale	60–90					S	S	S	S	S	S	S	
Kohlrabi	T: 45–60 S: 50–60					S	S	S	S	TS	TS	TS	T
Lettuce, Head	50–100					S	S	TS	TS	TS	TS	TS	TS
Lettuce, Leaf	50–90					S	S	TS	TS	TS	TS	TS	TS
Leek	180–200					S	S	S	S				
Melon, Musk Cantaloupe	80–120	S	S										
Melon, Watermelon	90–120												
Mustard Greens	35–45					S	S	S	S	S	S	S	S
Okra	70–100												
Onions, Bulb	S: 7–8 mon. Sets: 4-5 mon.								S	S	S		
Onions, Green	90–100				S	S	S	S	S	S	S	S	S
Parsnips	100–120							S	S				
Peanuts	5 months												
Peas	Sep: 60–120 Nov: 120–150						S	S	S	S	S	S	S
Peppers	90–120	T	T										
Potatoes	90–120												

S Seeds **T** Transplants

Planting Calendar—Fruits & Vegetables
July–December

Fruit or Vegetable	Days to Harvest	Jul 1	Jul 15	Aug 1	Aug 15	Sep 1	Sep 15	Oct 1	Oct 15	Nov 1	Nov 15	Dec 1	Dec 15
Potatoes, Sweet	120–160												
Pumpkin	90–120	S	S										
Radishes	40–60					S	S	S	S	S	S	S	S
Rutabagas	100–120							S	S	S	S		
Spinach	40–90					S	S	S	S	S	S	S	S
Squash, Summer	60–90				S								
Squash, Winter	90–120			S									
Tomatoes	50–120			T	T								
Turnips	90–120					S	S	S	S	S	S	S	S

S Seeds **T** Transplants

Planting Calendar—Herbs

Herb	Propagation Method			Type of Plant			When to Plant		
	Seed	Cutting	Division	Annual	Perennial	Biennial	Feb–Apr	Oct–Nov	Dec–Jan
Anise	✔			✗			♦	♦	
Basil	✔			✗			♦		
Bay[1]		✔			✗		♦		
Borage	✔			✗				♦	♦
Caraway	✔					✗	♦	♦	
Catnip	✔		✔		✗		♦	♦	♦
Chamomile	✔			✗			♦		♦
Chervil	✔			✗				♦	
Chives	✔		✔		✗		♦	♦	♦
Cilantro/ Coriander	✔			✗				♦	♦
Curry		✔			✗		♦		
Dill	✔			✗				♦	♦
Epazote	✔				✗		♦		
Fennel	✔			✗			♦	♦	♦
Fennel (Bulb)			✔		✗			♦	♦
Feverfew	✔	✔			✗		♦		♦
French Tarragon			✔		✗		♦		
Garlic (Clove)			✔	✗				♦	
Garlic Chives			✔		✗		♦	♦	♦
Germander		✔			✗		♦		
Horehound	✔	✔			✗		♦	♦	♦

Planting Calendar—Herbs

Herb	Propagation Method			Type of Plant			When to Plant		
	Seed	Cutting	Division	Annual	Perennial	Biennial	Feb–Apr	Oct–Nov	Dec–Jan
Hyssop	✔				✗		◆		
Lavender	✔	✔			✗		◆	◆	◆
Lemon Balm	✔	✔	✔		✗		◆	◆	
Lemon Grass			✔		✗		◆		
Lemon Verbena		✔			✗		◆		
Marjoram	✔	✔			✗		◆	◆	
Mint	✔	✔			✗		◆	◆	
Oregano	✔	✔			✗		◆	◆	
Parsley	✔					✗	◆	◆	◆
Rosemary		✔			✗			◆	◆
Rue		✔			✗		◆		
Safflower	✔			✗			◆		
Sage	✔	✔			✗		◆	◆	
Salad Burnet	✔				✗		◆	◆	
Santolina	✔	✔			✗		◆	◆	
Savory (Winter)	✔	✔			✗		◆	◆	
Savory (Summer)	✔	✔		✗			◆		
Scented Geraniums	✔	✔			✗		◆	◆	
Tansy			✔		✗		◆		
Thyme	✔	✔	✔		✗		◆	◆	◆
Yarrow	✔		✔		✗		◆	◆	

[1]Bay may take 6–8 months to propagate.

THE UNIVERSITY OF ARIZONA COOPERATIVE EXTENSION
Flower and Bedding Plant Guide for the Low Desert

Flower attributes, special characteristics and colors

Flower common & botanical names	Time to First Bloom (days from seed)	Height (inches unless noted other)	Difficulty	Light Needs	Water Needs	Hummingbirds	Seed-eating Bird	Butterflies	Edible	Good Cut Flower	Good For Drying	Wildflower ✓	Reseeds	Fragrance	BLUE	PURPLE	RED	PINK	ORANGE	YELLOW	WHITE
African Daisy (A) *Dimorphotheca sinuata*	120	4-12	E	B	L								x						x	x	x
Ageratum (A) *Ageratum houstonianum*	180	4-12	E	P	H										x	x					x
Arctotis, dwarf (A) *Arctotis acaulis*	135	10-12	E	B	L													x	x	x	x
Arctotis, tall (A) *Arctosis hybrid*	135	24-30	E	B	L								x				x	x	x	x	x
Asters (A) *Callistephus chinensis*	180	12-24	D	BP	H					x						x	x	x			x
Baby's Breath (A) *Gypsophila elegans*	160	18-30	M	B	M					x	x							x			x
Balsam (summer) (A) *Impatiens balsamina*	120	12-18	MD	BP	H				x							x	x	x			x
Bee Balm (P) *Monarda didyma*	75	24-36	D	P	H	x								x			x	x			x
Begonia (A) *Begonia x semperflorens-cultorum*	180	10-12	E	SP	H												x	x			x
Bells of Ireland (A) *Moluccella laevis*	180	18-24	E	B	LM					x	x		x								
Bigelow's Purple Aster (A) *Aster bigelovii*	150	24-36	E	B	M					x		x	x		x						
Bishop's Weed (A) *Ammi majus*	180	26-60	E	B	LM					x	x	x	x								x
Black-eyed Susan (A) *Rudbeckia hirta*	120	24-36	E	B	M		x	x		x		x							x	x	
Butterfly Weed (P) *Asclepias tuberosa* **	150	24-36	E	B	L	x		x		x			x						x	x	
Calendula (A) *Calendula officinalis*	100	15-18	E	B	M				x	x									x	x	
Candytuft (A) (Hyacinth-flowered) *Iberis amara*	135	12-18	E	BP	H					x				x				x			x
Candytuft (A) (Iberis) *Iberis sempervirens*	135	12	E	BP	H					x				x							x
Carnation (P) *Dianthus caryophyllus*	150	12-14	E	BP	M				x	x				x		x	x	x		x	x
Celosia (A) (Cockscomb) *Celosia cristata*	120	12-30	M	B	L					x	x					x	x	x	x	x	x

Planting & Flowering Guide (P = Planting, F = Flowering, L = Colorful Foliage/Fruit)

Flower	Jan	Feb	Mar	Apr	May	Jun	Jul	Aug	Sep	Oct	Nov	Dec
African Daisy	F	F F	F F	F F					P	P P	P P	P P
Ageratum	F	F F	F F	F F	F				P	P P	P P	P P
Arctotis, dwarf		F	F F	F F	F F	P				P	P P	P P
Arctotis, tall		F	F F	F F	F F	P				P	P P	P P
Asters	F	F F	F F	F F	F F	F				P	P P	P P
Baby's Breath	F	F	F F	F F	F					P	P P	P P
Balsam (summer)					P P	F F	F F	F				
Bee Balm				P	P F	F F	F F	F	F			
Begonia	F	F	F F	F F	F F	P P			F	F	F P	P
Bells of Ireland			P	P F	F F	F F				P	P	P
Bigelow's Purple Aster			P	P	P	P	F F	F	F F	F F/P	F P	P
Bishop's Weed			P	P F	F F	F F	F		F	F/P	F P	F/P
Black-eyed Susan	P	P	P	F	F	F F	F F	F	F	F	F	F
Butterfly Weed	F	F	P	P F	F F	F F	F F	F	F	F/P	P	L
Calendula	F F	F F	F F	F F	F F					P	P P	P P
Candytuft (H)		F	F F	F F	F F					P	P P	P P
Candytuft (I)		F	F F	F F	F F					P	P P	P P
Carnation	P	P P	P	F	F F					P	P P	P
Celosia			P	P	P P	F F	F F	F F	F F/P	F P/p	F Pp	F Pp

Keys

Plant Type
A = Annual - blooms & dies in one season ✓✓
B = Biennial - blooms & dies in second season
P = Perennial - Blooms more than two seasons

Light Needs
B = Bright Full Sun
P = Partial Sun
S = Shade

Difficulty
E = Easy to grow
M = Moderately easy to grow
D = Difficult to grow

Water Needs
H = High Water Use
M = Moderate Water Use
L = Low Water Use

Notes
* = Foliage Plant
** = Poisonous
*** = Very Difficult

Planting & Flowering Key
P = Planting Months
F = Flowering Months
L = Colorful Foliage/Fruit

Flower — Planting & Flowering Guide

Flower (common & botanical names)	Time to First Bloom (days from seed)	Height (inches unless noted)	Light Needs	Difficulty	Water Needs
Clarkia (A) *Clarkia amoena*	150	15-24	B	E	H
Coleus (A) *Coleus x hybridus* *	135	8-14	S	E	H
Coral Bells (A) *Heuchera sanguinea*	160	12-24	S	E	H
Coreopsis (A) *Coreopsis spp.*	30-60	12-30	B	E	M
Cornflower (A) (Bachelor's Button) *Centaurea cyanus*	120	18-30	B	E	M
Cosmos (A) *Cosmos bipinnatus*	120	36-72	B	E	L
Cosmos (yellow) (A) *Cosmos sulphureus*	120	36-48	B	E	LM
Dahlias (A) *Dahlia x hybrida*	45	12-36	P	D	H
Delphinium (A) *Delphinium x cultorum*	150	30-60	BP	M	M
Desert Marigold (A) *Baileya multiradiata*	180	12-18	B	E	L
Desert Milkweed (P) *Asclepias subulata* **	150	24-48	B	E	L
Desert Zinnia (A) *Zinnia acerosa*	180	12	B	D	L
Dianthus (A) (Sweet William) *Dianthus barbatus*	150	10-20	BP	E	M
Dusty Miller (P) *Senecio cineraria* *	N/A	8-16	B	E	L
English Daisy (A) *Bellis perennis*	120	6	S	E	H
Evening Primrose (P) *Oenothera berlandieri*	180	10-12	B	E	L
Flax (scarlet) (A) *Linum grandiflorum*	120	18-36	B	E	L
Flax (blue) (P) *Linum perenne lewisii*	120	18-24	B	E	M
Flowering Tobacco (A) *Nicotiana alata* **	180	12-30	P	M	M
Forget-Me-Not (A) *Myosotis sylvatica*	180	10-12	P	M	H
Four O'Clock (A) *Mirabilis jalapa* **	90	18-30	P	EM	L

Legends

Plant Type
A = Annual - blooms & dies in one season ✓
B = Biennial - blooms & dies in second season
P = Perennial - Blooms more than two seasons

Light Needs
B = Bright Full Sun
P = Partial Sun
S = Shade

Difficulty
E = Easy to grow
M = Moderately easy to grow
D = Difficult to grow

Water Needs
H = High Water Use
M = Moderate Water Use
L = Low Water Use

Notes
* = Foliage Plant
** = Poisonous
*** = Very Difficult

Planting & Flowering Key
P = Planting Months
F = Flowering Months
L = Colorful Foliage/Fruit

Planting & Flowering Guide

Flower common & botanical names	Time to First Bloom (days from seed)	Height (inches unless noted other)	Light Needs	Difficulty	Water Needs
Foxglove (A) *Digitalis purpurea* **	150	24-36	P	H	H
Gaillardia (P) (Blanket Flower) *Gaillardia grandiflora*	150	15-24	B	E	L
Gaillardia (A) (Blanket Flower) *Gaillardia pulchella*	150	15-24	B	E	L
Gazania (P) *Gazania x hybrida*	30-60	6-12	B	EM	L
Geranium (P) *Pelargonium x hortorum*	150	12-18	P	E	H
Gilia (A) *Gilia capitata*	60	8-30	B	M	L
Globe Amaranth (A) *Gomphrena globosa*	100	15-24	B	E	L
Globe Mallow (P) *Sphaeralcea ambigua*	120	24-36	B	E	L
Gloriosa Daisy (A) *Rudbeckia hirta* cv. Gloriosa	60	18-30	B	E	L
Hollyhock (A/B) *Alcea rosea*	180	36-72	B	E	M
Impatiens (A) *Impatiens walleriana*	90	6-12	S	M	H
Indian Paintbrush (A) *Castilleja chromosa* ***	165	24-30	B	D	L
Johnny-Jump-Up (A) *Viola tricolor*	120	4-6	P	E	M
Jupiter's Beard (P) *Centranthus ruber*	180	36	BP	E	LM
Kochia (A) (Summer Cypress) *Kochia scoparia* *	N/A	24-30	B	E	M
Larkspur (A) *Consolida ambigua*	180	24-48	B	E	LM
Linaria (A) (Toadflax) *Linaria maroccana*	180	12-15	B	E	M
Lisianthus (A) *Eustoma grandiflorum*	60-90	12-24	B	M	L
Lobelia (A) *Lobelia erinus*	150	6-10	P	E	H
Lupine (A) *Lupinus spp.*	120	6-10	PB	M	H

Legends

Plant Type
A = Annual - blooms & dies in one season ✔✔
B = Biennial - blooms & dies in second season
P = Perennial - Blooms more than two seasons

Light Needs
B = Bright Full Sun
P = Partial Sun
S = Shade

Difficulty
E = Easy to grow
M = Moderately easy to grow
D = Difficult to grow

Water Needs
H = High Water Use
M = Moderate Water Use
L = Low Water Use

Notes
* = Foliage Plant
** = Poisonous
*** = Very Difficult

Planting & Flowering Key
P = Planting Months
F = Flowering Months
L = Colorful Foliage/Fruit

Planting & Flowering Guide

Flower — common & botanical names	Time to First Bloom (days from seed)	Height (inches unless noted other)	Light Needs	Difficulty	Water Needs
Marigold, American/African (A) *Tagetes erecta*	30-60	18-36	B	E	H
Marigold, French (A) *Tagetes patula*	30-60	8-10	B	E	H
Mexican Hat (A) *Ratibida columnifera*	180	10-18	B	E	LM
Mexican Sunflower (A) *Tithonia rotundifolia*	120	48-96	B	E	L
Mignonette (A) *Reseda odorata*	120	8-12	P	M	LM
Nasturtiums (A) *Tropaeolum majus*	120	10-18	B	E	M
Nemesia (A) *Nemesia strumosa*	90	8-10	B	E	M
Nierembergia (A) *Nierembergia hippomanica violacea*	150	4-15	PB	E	M
Ornamental Cabbage/Kale (A) *Brassica oleracea* *	N/A	8-12	PB	E	H
Ornamental Pepper (A) *Capsicum annum***	90-120	8-12	PB	E	H
Painted Daisy (A) *Chrysanthemum coccineum*	150	18-24	B	M	H
Pansies (A) *Viola x wittrockiana*	30	6-12	P	E	M
Penstemon (P) (Firecracker) *Penstemon eatoni*	150	12-24	B	EM	L
Penstemon (P) (Parry's) *Penstemon parryi*	150	12-36	B	EM	L
Penstemon (P) (Desert Beardtongue) *P. pseudospectabilis*	150	12-24	B	EM	L
Periwinkle (Vinca) (A) *Catharanthus roseus*	30	8-18	B	E	H
Petunia (A) *Petunia x hybrida*	30	12-24	BP	E	MH
Phlox (A) *Phlox drummondii*	150	6-18	BP	E	M
Pincushion Flower (A) *Scabiosa spp.*	180	18-30	B	EM	M
Poppy, California (A) *Eschscholzia californica*	150	6-12	B	E	L

Special Characteristics

Lures: Hummingbirds, Seed-eating Brds, Butterflies; Edible; Good Cut Flower; Good For Drying; Wildflower; Reseeds; Fragrance

Colors

Blue, Purple, Red, Pink, Orange, Yellow, White

Plant Type
A = Annual - blooms & dies in one season ✔
B = Biennial - blooms & dies in second season
P = Perennial - blooms more than two seasons

Light Needs
B = Bright Full Sun
P = Partial Sun
S = Shade

Difficulty
E = Easy to grow
M = Moderately easy to grow
D = Difficult to grow

Water Needs
H = High Water Use
M = Moderate Water Use
L = Low Water Use

Notes
* = Foliage Plant
** = Poisonous
*** = Very Difficult

Planting & Flowering Key
P = Planting Months
F = Flowering Months
L = Colorful Foliage/Fruit

Planting & Flowering Guide

Flower Attributes

Flower common & botanical names	Time to First Bloom (days from seed)	Height (inches unless noted)	Light Needs	Difficulty	Water Needs
Poppy (A) Iceland *Papaver nudicaule*	120	12-24	B	E	LM
Poppy (A) Shirley *Papaver Rhoeas*	120	24-48	B	E	LM
Portulaca (A) *Portulaca grandiflora*	30	4-6	B	E	L
Purple Coneflower (A) *Echinacea purpurea*	180	24-48	B	E	LM
Primrose (A) Fairy *Primula malacoides*	120	6-14	S	M	M
Primrose (A) Polyanthus *Primula polyantha*	120	4-12	S	M	M
Purslane (A) *Portulaca x hybrida*	30	4-8	B	E	L
Ranunculus (P) *Ranunculus x hybridus*	120	8-18	B	E	MH
Safflower (A) *Carthamus tinctorius*	120	12-36	B	E	L
Sage (P) *Salvia spp.*	90	5-48	B	E	L
Salpiglosis (A) *Salpiglosis sinuata*	150	15-30	B	D	M
Salvia (A) *Salvia splendens*	30	15-30	BP	E	M
Sanvitalia (A) (Creeping zinnia) *Sanvitalia procumbens*	30	6-12	B	M	L
Schizanthus (A) *Schizanthus x wisetonensis*	150	18-24	S	H	H
Shasta Daisy (A) *Chrysanthemum maximum*	180	24-36	P	E	MH
Shungiku Chrysanthemum (A) *C. coronarium*	120	24-36	B	E	M
Snapdragon (A) *Antirrhinum majus*	30-60	6-36	B	E	M
Spider Flower (A) *Cleome spinosa*	180	48-60	B	E	L
Star Clusters (A) *Pentas lanceolata*	180	24-30	S	D	H
Statice (A) (Sea Lavender) *Limonium sinuatum*	150	18-24	B	E	L

Special Characteristics & Colors

Flower	Hummingbirds	Seed-eating Birds	Butterflies	Edible	Good Cut Flower	Good for Drying	Wildflower	Reseeds	Fragrance	Blue	Purple	Red	Pink	Orange	Yellow	White
Poppy Iceland									x				x	x	x	x
Poppy Shirley							x	x				x	x	x	x	x
Portulaca							x					x	x	x	x	x
Purple Coneflower		x	x						x		x	x	x			x
Primrose Fairy											x	x	x			x
Primrose Polyanthus				x							x	x	x	x	x	x
Purslane												x	x	x	x	x
Ranunculus					x						x	x	x	x	x	x
Safflower		x			x	x								x	x	
Sage	x				x				x		x	x	x			
Salpiglosis					x						x	x	x		x	x
Salvia	x		x		x				x		x	x	x			x
Sanvitalia															x	
Schizanthus			x								x	x	x			x
Shasta Daisy			x		x											x
Shungiku		x	x	x				x							x	
Snapdragon					x						x	x	x	x	x	x
Spider Flower			x								x		x			x
Star Clusters		x									x	x	x			x
Statice					x	x				x	x		x		x	x

Planting & Flowering Months (P = Planting, F = Flowering, L = Colorful Foliage/Fruit)

Flower	Jan	Feb	Mar	Apr	May	Jun	Jul	Aug	Sep	Oct	Nov	Dec
Poppy Iceland	P	P	F	F	F					P	P	P
Poppy Shirley	P	F	F	F	F					P	P	P
Portulaca			P	F	F/P	F/P	F	F	F	F/P	F	
Purple Coneflower			F	F	F	F	F	F	F			
Primrose Fairy	P	P	F	F	F					P	P	P
Primrose Polyanthus	P	P	F	F	F					P	P	P
Purslane	P	P	F	F	F	F				P		
Ranunculus		P	P	F/P	F	F				P	P	P
Safflower			F	F	F	F	F	F	F	F		
Sage			F	F	F	F	F	F	F	F		
Salpiglosis			F	F	F	F	F	F	F	F		
Salvia			F	F	F	F	F	F	F	F	F	F
Sanvitalia				F	F	F	F	F	F			
Schizanthus				F/P	F/P	F	F					
Shasta Daisy				F	F	F	F	F				
Shungiku				F	F	F	F					
Snapdragon	F/P	F/P	F	F	F/P	F/P	F/P	F/P	F/P	F/P	F/P	F/P
Spider Flower				F	F	F	F	F	F	P	P	P
Star Clusters				F	F	F	F	F	F		P	P
Statice			F	F	F	F	F	F	F	F	F	F

Legends

Plant Type
A = Annual - blooms & dies in one season ✓✓
B = Biennial - blooms & dies in second season
P = Perennial - Blooms more than two seasons

Light Needs
B = Bright Full Sun
P = Partial Sun
S = Shade

Difficulty
E = Easy to grow
M = Moderately easy to grow
D = Difficult to grow

Water Needs
H = High Water Use
M = Moderate Water Use
L = Low Water Use

Notes
* = Foliage Plant
** = Poisonous
*** = Very Difficult

Planting & Flowering Key
P = Planting Months
F = Flowering Months
L = Colorful Foliage/Fruit

Planting & Flowering Guide

Flower common & botanical names	Time to First Bloom (days from seed)	Height (inches unless noted other)	Light Needs	Difficulty	Water Needs	Hummingbirds	Seed-eating Birds	Butterflies	Edible	Good Cut Flower	Good For Drying	Wildflower ✔	Reseeds	Fragrance	Blue	Purple	Red	Pink	Orange	Yellow	White
Stock (A) *Matthiola incana*	150	12-24	B	E	MH					X				X		X		X			X
Strawflower (A) *Helichrysum bracteatum*	150	12-36	B	D	L					X	X						X	X	X	X	X
Sunflower (A) *Helianthus annus*	90	36-60	B	E	M	X	X		X	X									X	X	X
Sweet Alyssum (A) *Lobularia maritima*	30	6-12	BP	E	MH			X						X		X		X			X
Sweet Peas (A) *Lathyrus odoratus*	120	12-72	B	E	H					X				X	X	X	X	X			X
Sweet Sultan (A) *Centaurea moschata*	150	30-36	B	E	M					X				X		X		X			X
Verbena (A) *Verbena peruviana*	120	6-8	B	E	M											X	X				
Verbena (A) *Verbena goodingii*	120	8-18	B	E	L			X				✔	X			X					
Violet (A) *Viola spp.*	135	4-6	P	E	M				X							X					
Wild Hyssop (P) *Agastache spp.*	90-210	24-36	BP	M	LM	X						✔		X	X			X			
Yarrow (P) *Achillea spp.*	30	12-24	B	E	L					X	X		X				X	X		X	X
Zinnia (A) *Zinnia elegans*	30	4-30	B	E	M					X							X	X	X	X	X

✔ Note: "Wildflowers", in this chart, refers to native annuals and other plants which are easily grown from seed and can naturalize by reseeding.
✔✔ Note: Many plants that are considered perennial in other growing climates, perform better as annuals in the low desert.

Plant Type	Light Needs	Difficulty	Water Needs	Notes	Planting & Flowering Key
A = Annual - blooms & dies in one season ✔✔	B = Bright Full Sun	E = Easy to grow	H = High Water Use	* = Foliage Plant	P = Planting Months
B = Biennial - blooms & dies in second season	P = Partial Sun	M = Moderately easy to grow	M = Moderate Water Use	** = Poisonous	F = Flowering Months
P = Perennial - Blooms more than two seasons	S = Shade	D = Difficult to grow	L = Low Water Use	*** = Very Difficult	L = Colorful Foliage/Fruit

Glossary

Acidic soil. Soil that has a pH reading below 7. See **pH**.

Alkaline soil. Soil that has a pH reading above 7. See **pH**.

Amendments. Any additives intended to enhance drainage, aeration, fertility and other properties of the soil.

Annuals. Plants whose life cycle (vegetative growth, bloom, seed set) is completed in a single growing season. At the end of a single growing season, the entire plant dies. A new generation begins each year with the germination of seeds.

Beneficial insects. Beneficials may be pollinators (e.g., honey bees), decomposers (e.g., sow bugs), parasites (e.g., parasitic wasps) or predators (e.g., lady beetles). Predators labeled as beneficials consume other insects that are considered to be pests. To complete their development, predators must eat large quantities of their prey and will often arrive on the scene if populations of their prey are available. Other predators include: praying mantises, dragonflies, green lacewings, assassin bugs and spiders.

Berm. A rim of soil built up around a plant or group of plants to hold in water and to capture salts as the water evaporates. Salts appear as white deposits on the soil's surface. The salts are kept away from the plant roots for that growing season and can be skimmed off the soil, if desired. Traditional Native American planting practices in the Southwest often included the use of some type of berm.

Bermuda grass. A fast-growing, tenacious lawn grass that readily spreads to nearby flower and vegetable beds.

Biennials. Plants with a life cycle of two years. Flowering and seed formation usually occur in the second year, followed by the death of the entire plant.

Biological control. A living plant, animal or organism that manages or limits the damage done by a pest or other undesirable condition in the garden.

Caliche. Found in some soils of the Southwest, caliche is an impervious layer consisting of calcium carbonate (lime). Many gardeners believe they have encountered caliche, but it is more likely to have been very hard-packed clay soil. See **Hardpan.**

Companion planting. The concept of placing together plants that benefit each other. A mutually beneficial planting scheme might include plants that fix nitrogen in the soil, provide a natural trellis, are thought to repel certain pests or attract beneficial insects.

Compost. Made from the decomposed remains of organic matter such as plants, grass clippings, kitchen scraps and manure. The more frequently that piles are watered and turned to aerate and mix, the more quickly organic matter will break down and be ready for use.

Cover crop. A cover crop is planted to improve the soil for the next season's crop. It may do this by breaking up the soil with its extensive root system, "fixing" nitrogen in the soil, and/or adding organic matter when the crop is tilled under.

Most legume crops can fix nitrogen. Examples of cover crops include alfalfa, beans, buckwheat, clover, peas and hairy vetch.

Crop rotation. The process of rotating the locations where specific crops, or families of crops, are planted each season. The process promotes soil fertility and deters the buildup of soil-borne diseases.

Cuttings. The propagation of new plants using growth from existing stock. In this book we are referring to softwood cuttings (other methods apply to shrubs or trees with hardwood). A stem is cut below a leaf during the growing season. After removing the lower leaves, the stem is dipped in a rooting hormone and planted in any medium with good water penetration and drainage. Some cuttings can be simply suspended in water and rooted.

Diatomaceous earth (DE). Tiny, fossilized silica shells that are mined to create an insecticidal powder. The microscopic silica shards cut into the insect as it moves through them; the insect eventually dies from dehydration. DE is not specific to any insect and will kill beneficials as well. The DE used in swimming pools is from the same source but is a different grade.

Division. The process of segmenting certain perennials and plants grown from rhizomes, bulbs or tubers which over time become crowded and therefore less vigorous. Pull or cut apart smaller clumps or individual plants during dormancy (fall for spring or early summer bloomers; spring for late summer and fall bloomers). Many perennial herbs can be propagated in this manner.

Drip irrigation. An efficient and water-saving system that uses thin "spaghetti" tubing with attached emitters to provide a slow, steady flow, or drip, of water.

Early. A plant variety that is planted "early" in the growing season and has a relatively shorter period of time to reach maturity.

Everlastings. Flowers grown for use in dried arrangements.

Fungal disease. Some fungi can parasitize plants. Fungi reproduce by spores, which can be transmitted by wind or water. Fungal diseases can be controlled by fungicides and careful cultural practices, e.g., watering near the base of the plant, not on the leaves.

Fungicide. An agent applied to plants or soil to kill or control a fungal disease.

Green manure. A plant grown specifically to produce bulk for compost.

Gypsum. A mineral, calcium sulfate, which is often added to alkaline Southwestern soil to improve the soil's structure. It pulls sodium away from soil particles and allows it to be washed away, thus helping water and air to move through the soil more effectively.

Harden off. The process of helping plants that have been started indoors, under cover or in a greenhouse, to survive outdoors in direct sun and wind. One way is to daily place the potted plants outdoors for increasing lengths of time one to two weeks before planting in the ground.

Hardpan. A hard layer found in some soils. Compacted, and often clayey, it hampers root penetration and drainage. See **Caliche.**

Hardy. Hardiness refers to a plant's ability to resist frost or freezing temperatures. A half-hardy plant may withstand some cold temperatures but will probably freeze if temperatures are severe.

Hardiness zone. Determined by the USDA based on average annual low temperature. Many other factors (altitude, wind, soil) can impact plant growth. Some garden reference works have their own, more detailed, zone mapping.

Heirloom. A plant variety that has been open-pollinated for at least three generations. That is, there has been no cross-pollination between varieties via human or other intervention. Thus, seeds will produce a replica of the parent plant.

Herbicide. An agent that kills plants.

Hybrid. Plants produced by the cross-pollination of two different parent varieties. Seeds from hybrid plants will not mature into plants identical to the parent.

Inorganic. Composed of material other than plant or animal.

Integrated pest management (IPM). IPM is a method for examining all options available for dealing with pests, including doing nothing at all. The use of pesticides is considered only after careful monitoring and lack of success with natural control factors. IPM allows the gardener to consider all options for the easiest, least costly and most environmentally friendly way to control pests.

Laser tubing. Drip irrigation tubing that has tiny, laser-generated holes spaced evenly along its length, allowing for even and efficient watering.

Late. A plant variety that is planted later in the growing season or requires more days to reach maturity, resulting in a harvest toward the end of the growing season.

Layering. A propagation method that roots a branch while it is attached to the parent plant. The parent provides nutrients until the branch forms its own roots.

Leaching. Usually refers to the application of enough water to the soil to move excess salt accumulations below the root zone. Unfortunately, nutrients can also be lost in this manner.

Macronutrients. These six nutrients are needed in fairly large amounts for healthy plant growth and development. Nitrogen, phosphorus and potassium often need to be added to soil in the form of fertilizers. Calcium, magnesium and sulfur may also need to be added, usually in the form of soil amendments such as gypsum (calcium sulfate).

Micronutrients. Sometimes called trace elements, these are needed for plant growth in addition to macronutrients. They usually exist in sufficient quantity in the soil, air and water, but may need to be supplemented. They are boron, chlorine, copper, iron, molybdenum, and zinc.

Mulch. Loose material placed over the soil to insulate it from rapid temperature changes, decrease water evaporation, deter weeds, prevent mud from splashing onto vegetation, feed the soil through decomposition and to increase the beauty of the garden. Mulch is usually thought of as organic (bark, sawdust, clippings, leaves), but small rock can also serve some of these purposes in ornamental beds.

Nematodes (Root Knot). Nematodes are microscopic roundworms. There are beneficial nematodes as well as harmful ones. Generally, we are referring to root knot nematodes that live in the soil and feed on plant roots, interfering with the plant's ability to take up water and nutrients. General failure to thrive can be a symptom of infestation; when the roots are examined, they appear to have warts if these nematodes are present.

Nitrogen. One of the three major elements required by plants, the others being phosphorus and potassium. Its chemical symbol is "N." Nitrogen promotes growth and a healthy green color.

Nutsedge. Sometimes called nutgrass, this perennial weed's bright green leaves are about 1/4-inch-wide and have a highly visible midvein. The roots have small tubers (nutlets) attached. It spreads vigorously by these tubers and by seeds.

Open-pollinated. Seeds produced from plants that were pollinated naturally via wind, insects or water. Plants of the same species often need to be kept separate if one plans to collect seeds, so that cross pollination (if not desirable) will not occur. For example, sweet peppers are usually kept in an area apart from hot peppers (chiles).

Organic matter. The decayed remains of formerly living plants or animals. Organic matter is incorporated into desert soils to improve drainage, aeration and fertility. It will not, however, provide all essential plant nutrients, nor are nutrients immediately available for the plant's use unless the material is well decomposed before application.

Perennials. Plants with a life cycle of two or more years. Some perennials will lose the top growth at the end of each growing season, but many perennial plants keep their foliage year round.

Perlite. A volcanic mineral that is heat-treated to puff up into lightweight white granules. It is often added to prepared potting soil mixtures to provide aeration and drainage in the soil.

Permeability. A measure of how readily soil allows a liquid or gas to flow through.

Pesticide. An agent that kills a pest.

pH. A measure of the soil's acidity or alkalinity, rated on a logarithmic scale from 0–14; 7.0 is neutral, lower numbers are acidic and higher numbers are alkaline. Southwestern soils are typically alkaline.

Phosphorus. One of the three major elements required by plants, the others being nitrogen and potassium. Its chemical symbol is "P." Among other things, phosphorus promotes flower and fruit production.

Potassium. One of the three major elements required by plants, the others being nitrogen and phosphorus. Its chemical symbol is "K." Potassium promotes hardiness, vigor and disease resistance. There is generally ample potassium available in alkaline soils so there is no need to add it.

PVC (polyvinyl chloride) pipe. White, lightweight plastic pipe often used for irrigation systems.

Rhizome. A thick modified stem. A rhizome grows horizontally under the soil surface, producing new growth as it extends. Examples of plants that spread with rhizomes are nutsedge, iris and violets. See **Stolon.**

Root bound. When plants have grown beyond the capacity of their containers, the roots will begin to circle around the inside of the pot, eventually circling back onto themselves. Root-bound plants can only be grown successfully if the encircling roots are untangled or cut before planting in the ground.

Side dress. The application of supplemental nutrients to the soil above the plant's root zone, away from the stem to avoid burning.

Soaker hose. A hose that "weeps" water along its entire length, allowing for slow, even soaking.

Soil structure. The manner in which the soil's basic elements are bonded together and the resulting amount of pore space between the particles; that is, its permeability or ability to retain water and nutrients.

Soil sulfur. A naturally occurring mineral used to lower alkalinity in the soil.

Soil texture. The relative proportions of sand, silt and clay particles that make up soil.

Solarization. A process designed to kill disease, nematodes and weed seeds by pasteurizing or heating the top six or so inches of soil. In early summer, prepare the bed for fall planting and then cover with clear plastic for several weeks. Do not recultivate soil before planting as there is a risk of bringing untreated soil into the growing zone.

Square foot gardening. A method of intensive gardening that is based on densely planting in one-foot-square grids, creating savings in space, water, labor and amendments. The principle is to create beds that are small enough to be worked from the side so that no time or money is spent amending soil that will be used as a path and so the gardener never steps on the planting beds.

Stolon. A stolon is a creeping stem, above ground, that roots along the path of growth and sends up a new plant at each place it roots. Examples of plants that spread by stolons are Bermuda grass and strawberries. See **Rhizome.**

Systemic. Any chemical that a plant absorbs and distributes throughout its system to kill a pest or the plant itself.

Thinning. The removal of plants so that the remaining seedlings are spaced at a distance that will provide adequate growing room. Distances are usually provided on the seed packet.

Treated seeds. Seeds that have been treated to aid germination, prevent disease or provide some other beneficial feature. Most treated seeds are color-coated.

Untreated seeds. Seeds that have not been coated with fungicides or undergone other kinds of special treatments.

Vermiculite. A mineral, mica, is heated, causing it to puff up to form lightweight granules of vermiculite. Used in potting soils to improve water retention and aeration.

Index

For More Information

Maricopa County Cooperative Extension
Main Office Master Gardener Hotline
Phone (602) 827-8200, ext. 301
8:00 a.m. - 5 p.m., Monday-Friday
Located between 40th and 48th Streets
4341 E. Broadway Road
Phoenix, AZ 85040-8807

Master Gardener Satellite Offices
Northwest Valley Satellite Office
Phone (623) 546-1672
Call for days and hours
Located at Property Owners and
    Residents Association (PORA) Building
13815 Camino del Sol
Sun City West, AZ 85375

East Valley Satellite Office
Phone (480) 985-0338
Call for days and hours
Located at the Red Mountain
    Multi-Generational Center
7550 East Adobe
Mesa, Arizona   85207

Northeast Valley Satellite Office
Phone (480) 312-5810
Call for days and hours
Located at the Via Linda Senior Center
10440 East Via Linda
Scottsdale, Arizona 85258

Web site: http://cals.arizona.edu/maricopa/garden/

Acknowledgements

We would like to thank the following people for generously sharing their time and their extensive knowledge of desert gardening with us:

Arizona Herb Association: Mike Hills and Kirti Matura

City of Mesa Water Resources Division: Donna DiFrancesco

City of Phoenix Water Resources: Kent Newland

Flower Gardener Extraordinaire: Cindy Smith

Maricopa County (Arizona) Master Gardeners: Cheryl Czaplicki, Roberta Gibson, Frank Martin, Olin Miller, Erin O'Dell, Carole Palmer, Mary Rider and Annette Weaver

Maricopa County Cooperative Extension: Carolyn Chard, Shanyn Hosier, Joanne Littlefield, Cathy Munger and Cathy Rymer

Permaculture Drylands Institute: Brandy Winters

The University of Arizona: Terry Mikel, Commercial Horticulture Agent; Kai Umeda, Vegetable Crops Agent; and Deborah J. Young, Associate Director, Programs

Wild Seeds: Rita Jo Anthony

About the Authors

Cathy Cromell is an Editor at The University of Arizona Maricopa County Cooperative Extension in Phoenix. She practices organic gardening and is a certified Master Gardener, Master Entomologist and Master Composter. She is a contributing writer for *Phoenix Home & Garden* magazine.

Linda A. Guy is a Master Gardener and a member of the International Aromatherapy and Herb Association. Her gardening interests include growing herbs and studying their use in herbal remedies. She assists with garden and landscape projects at her children's school.

Lucy K. Bradley was the Urban Horticulture Agent for the University of Arizona Maricopa County Cooperative Extension in Phoenix. She is now Assistant Professor with North Carolina State University.

Order Form

Desert Gardening for Beginners @ $8.95 $_____

Desert Landscaping for Beginners @ $14.95 $_____

Desert Water Gardening for Beginners @ $17.95 $_____

Earth-Friendly Desert Gardening @ *14.95* $_____

Add $5 shipping/handling for each copy $_____

TOTAL ENCLOSED $_____

Name   _____

Address   _____

City, State, Zip   _____

Phone   _____

Email   _____

Send check payable to University of Arizona, Arizona Master
Gardener Press, 4341 E. Broadway Road, Phoenix, AZ 85040-8807.
For book details, go to http://cals.arizona.edu/maricopa/garden